THE FRIENDS OF JOE GILMORE

AND

SOME FRIENDS OF LYLE SAXON

LYLE SAXON AND JOE GILMORE — *Madison Street House,*
French Quarter, New Orleans

BY LYLE SAXON

The Friends of Joe Gilmore

A N D

Some Friends of Lyle Saxon

BY EDWARD DREYER

With fourteen illustrations including six

reproductions of pencil sketches by

E. H. SUYDAM

A FIREBIRD PRESS BOOK

PELICAN PUBLISHING COMPANY
Gretna 1998

Manufactured in the United States of America
Published by Pelican Publishing Company, Inc.
1000 Burmaster Street, Gretna, Louisiana 70053

Contents

[v]

Contents

Illustrations

Foreword

Lyle Saxon died before he was able to finish this semi-autobiographical book. Most of it he dictated during his illness.

The late E. H. Suydam, who illustrated three of Saxon's earlier books, made the drawings, here reproduced, especially for Saxon while preparing drawings for *Fabulous New Orleans* and *Old Louisiana*.

Whenever Saxon's telephone rang, and it rang incessantly, if the caller announced that he was a friend or a friend of friends, Saxon's stock answer was: "Friends? What friends? I haven't any friends." Few men have had more. My own notes, therefore, make no pretense at being all inclusive. In collecting them I have become indebted to a number of people, who set me straight on certain points or refreshed my memory on others, but especially to Henry Alsberg, Hazel Breaux, Ann Christmas, Tess Crager, Judith Hyams Douglas, Irma Fastnacht, Weeks Hall, Marjory Hunter, Dora Thea Hettwer, the late Dorothy Johnston, Alberta Kinsey, Clair Laning, Joel Lawrence, Olive Lyons, Leo Spofford, Noel Straus, and Robert Tallant.

E. D.

New York

THE FRIENDS OF JOE GILMORE

CHAPTER I

Joe Takes Over

Never will I forget the day I first met Joe Gilmore. There was an office full of people, and I was trying to get a lot of personnel affairs straightened out, when in at the door came a black boy with a great, wide smile and beautiful teeth.

"Mr. Saxon," he said, "I got to have a job."

"But I have no job," I said. "What can you do? This is not the kind of an office where I can employ you."

"That don't matter; I got to have a job."

At the time, I was suffering with neuritis—pains in the neck, shoulders, and arms. I could not even get my hand up to tie my necktie. A thought occurred to me.

"What can you do, Joe?" I asked.

"I can do anything," he said.

"How about massage?" I asked. "Can you do that too?"

"Yassuh."

"Very well," I said. "Come to my room at the hotel at eight o'clock this evening and bring a bottle of rubbing alcohol with you."

I came home so miserable I was ready to die; I did not even have dinner. I undressed and lay on the bed, and pretty soon Joe appeared with a bottle in his hand.

"Well, start off," I said, "because God knows I feel like hell."

And Joe, at the first gesture, slapped me with a hand hard as cement, practically killing me.

I screamed, and said, "Joe! do you know anything about massage?"

And he said, "You teach me."

So I taught Joe to give me an alcohol rub and massage that did not hurt too much.

I kept him on my own payroll after that. I don't know why. But he was there day in and day out. Some days I had neuritis and some days I didn't; but it did not matter. He was so amusing.

He said, "I likes working for you."

I was living at the St. Charles Hotel in New Orleans. Joe would come around, clean the room, and give orders to the maids—which made them mad. He became our superintendent and our boss. My job was hard, but when I came home, there was Joe with his big, wide smile. He made it not too hard a life.

A little later, I got hold of some money from Cecil B. DeMille for the motion picture rights to *Lafitte, the Pirate*, which was filmed as "The Buccaneer," and when the receipts came in, I decided to buy another old house in the French Quarter which might be restored. So I bought the house—a very beautiful house on Madison Street, which is a little street extending from Chartres to Decatur. The house was of the Spanish type. It was practically a shell and needed tremendous remodeling. Joe worked with me. I asked him to stay on the job while the house was being repaired. We had architects, contractors, and workmen. The place was filthy and had to be done from top to bottom, from roof to floors; but it was so beautiful, it was worthwhile. On one side were Spanish arches—three above and three on the ground which opened into sort of a loggia paved with flagstones. I had looked this over and liked it. It was a place where I wanted to sit and drink.

On one of the first days, while I was sitting looking at the wreckage and wondering if I would ever be able to make it into a real house, Joe appeared and said, "Mr. Saxon, what you need is a Suisse."

"Well, fix me one," I said.

So he turned up a few minutes later with two glasses of dripped absinthe, and as I sat looking at all the debris in the courtyard, I kept recalling the words of a song from an old musical comedy. They were:

> At the first cool sip on your fevered lip,
> You determine to live through the day;
> Life's again worthwhile, as with dawning smile
> You imbibe your absinthe frappé.

"Joe," I said, "how did you make this?"

He said, "Mr. Saxon, I just found your old absinthe dripper, and I knows how to do it."

We drank the absinthe. In some funny way the world looked better.

[5]

The beautiful house became more complicated than I had feared. Old problems, which I had not really anticipated, arose. One was garbage. In the French Quarter there are no alleys, and garbage must be picked up and put out in front. So I bought four garbage cans. Joe brought them down and explained to the people in the house—four families—that the garbage must be collected and taken out. I was planting sweet olive trees and I wanted the house to smell of sweet olive, not of garbage. I left the management entirely to Joe. He got in touch with a colored man named Magee who had a truck. Magee tried to chisel his way in, saying, "I am your new trash boy."

"After all," I said, "I have Joe working for me, and you will have to work through him because that's the way it is."

I did not realize that this was starting a feud between Joe and Magee. One day as I was wandering around the lower floor of this enormous house—eighteen rooms—I came near a front window opening out on Madison Street and heard an altercation. Joe was giving orders. Magee turned to him and said, "O.K., Black Saxon."

I knew then this was a lifetime friendship between Joe and me.

From this time on, I think, Joe took over; and his wife Alma, pretty, pleasant, black, and fat, came to cook for me. Joe was major-domo, valet, butler, and yardman. The house was so large that I was unable to live in it as I had thought I would. I had originally intended to live upstairs, have the servants' quarters downstairs on one side of the courtyard and my office on the other; but this was not to be.

[6]

LYLE SAXON IN THE COURTYARD OF THE MADISON STREET HOUSE

One day in the St. Charles Hotel, where I was still living, I fell flat on my face with a ruptured appendix. Eddie Dreyer carried me to the Baptist Hospital for an operation. It was more serious than I think anyone had anticipated; so instead of moving into the house, I kept one apartment there and continued to live at the Hotel. But the house was so attractive that when friends came to town some stayed there.

Howard Hunter and his wife rented the lower apartment which had the arches. Their friends began to arrive, and most of them were very amusing. Life began to be amusing too, though I still lived at the Hotel. Hunter's wife, Marge, was one of the nicest women I have ever met in my life, and her parties were very good because we continued to play jokes upon each other.

Around the corner on Toulouse Street lived Roark Bradford, writer of Negro stories, and his wife Mary Rose, of whom I will speak more later. Bradford and I were old friends; we had worked together as reporters on the *Times-Picayune*.

The Bradfords had two excellent servants, colored women, whose names were Louise and Lucille, or 'Cile. They were very pretty and very light. One day as I was walking just in front of St. Louis Cathedral, I met 'Cile. She was coming back from the French Market, which was right around the corner. When she saw me, she said, "Mr. Saxon, that man of yours, Mr. Gilmore—I has a razor in my garter and I'm goin' to kill him if I live, and when I sees him again, I'm goin' to cut him up."

"Why, 'Cile?" I asked.

She said, "He come in the kitchen at the Bradford's house and took liberties."

I said, "What did he do, 'Cile?"

"I ain't goin' to tell you," she said, "but he took liberties, and I'm goin' to kill him."

I thought about this, so I said, " 'Cile, if you and Joe have had some kind of trouble between you, you are going to have to adjust it yourselves. After all, what can I do?"

Just then the Cathedral clock chimed four o'clock in the afternoon and I added, " 'Cile, if you have already been to the market, why not come home with me? Joe is going to make me a drink, and I would be glad to have you come along, if you care to. Then we can talk this over."

'Cile said, "I hates that man, and if I meets him, I'm goin' to kill him with this razor."

"All right 'Cile, I have said all I have to say, and this is the end of it as far as I am concerned."

So I went to the house on Madison Street, and Joe was there with his wife. I sat under the arches in the courtyard, and yelled, "Joe, for God's sake, get me a drink."

And he said, "How would you like a Sazerac?"

It was delicious, and I had three, which is too many.

In the meantime, Joe had turned on the hose and was cleaning the courtyard. He had taken off his shoes and was running around barefooted. I wanted to take off my shoes and run around barefooted too, but instead, I sat and drank those delectable Sazeracs.

A week later, exactly in front of St. Louis Cathedral, as before, I met 'Cile. She was like a mourning dove. She looked at me and said, "Mr. Saxon, how's Joseph?"

"Well," I said, "a week ago I met you here, and you wanted to kill Joe. Why are you worrying about him now?"

She said, "You can't stay mad with a man who's got a hundred teeth."

I went over to Jackson Square and thought about it, and realized that something had happened I could do nothing about. So I went home and asked Joe to make me another Sazerac.

CHAPTER II

Katie and Gwyn Speak Their Pieces

During this time I was editing a series of guide books and I had two pleasant people working with me. I still remember how lucky I was. One was Eddie Dreyer, who was my assistant and took charge of the office in my absence. The other was a red-headed girl, Katie Cassibry, who was my secretary and was one of the most amusing people I have ever known. There was hardly a day she didn't come to the office with some funny story to tell me. Of course both of them knew Joe Gilmore—and Joe Gilmore knew them.

Once we had a great deal of work to do checking tours on the left bank of the Mississippi River. Other people had compiled and checked the material, but we felt that it should be rechecked before the book went to press. So we got a car which Joe Gilmore drove. I sat in the front with him. Katie and Eddie sat on the back seat. It was really a gruelling job. Katie had her notebook, Eddie had the manuscript which we were correcting, and I, who knew the country, watched for what we then called "points of interest." We were all bored and very tired. The work had been very hard. For example, we would say, "Let's see what this is, 10.6 miles from Donaldsonville." The manuscript would read: "At the left you will see a ruined sugar mill. If you leave the main road and go two miles to the right, you will come to a shrine of St. Amico." So we would turn off the highway and go two miles to the right, just to make sure.

Our tempers were wearing thin. We were beginning to be cross with each other. Only Joe Gilmore was all smiles.

As we reached some sort of manufacturing plant, we saw a large pile of celotex, which is a sort of insulation board manufactured from the residue of sugar cane. It was piled up in the shape of a barn, covered with a tarpaulin. Katie leaned out the car window and said, "What is that?"

I replied crossly, "Katie! You have been in Louisiana half of your life; so don't tell me you don't know what that is. It is a wall-board; it is made from the dried sugar cane stalks that are called *bagasse*."

I suppose I spoke more crossly than I realized. There was complete silence in the car.

We had driven perhaps half a mile further and it was beginning to get dark. Suddenly I saw something on the road and called, "Watch out, Joe! What's that?" It turned out to be only a cow but Katie turned to Eddie and said, "The trouble with Papa is that he doesn't know his *bagasse* from a hole in the ground," which brought us all into laughter and broke the tension.

Joe Gilmore said, "Mr. Saxon, don't you think we ought to stop at the next saloon and get us all a *bagasse* cocktail?"

"For heaven's sake," I said, "What's that?"

"I shows you when we gets there," said Joe.

[11]

So we stopped at the next bar and had our bagasse cocktail. It was plain Bourbon and soda; but we all felt better.

In our office there also worked a nice boy named Joseph Treadaway. He came to us as office boy and worked up to office manager. He had been with us for a number of years, and had seen people come and go, but apparently had no great interest in them. But when he heard me speak over the phone to Mary Rose Bradford, saying I was coming to dinner with John Steinbeck, Treadaway said, "Mr. Saxon, I have never asked you anything before, but I think John Steinbeck's book, *The Grapes of Wrath,* is the best book I have ever read. I would give anything in the world if I could just see Mr. Steinbeck."

"Well, Treadaway," I said, "I think that can be arranged. I will take you down with me, give you a drink, and let you meet Mr. Steinbeck. You can stay about half an hour, because as you know Mrs. Bradford has her dinner party already planned."

He said, "Mr. Saxon, I will do exactly that."

So off we went.

My old friend, Roark Bradford, had taken his little son, Richard, to Sarasota, Florida, to see the circus at winter quarters. Just at this time John Steinbeck arrived in New Orleans, bringing with him Miss Gwyn Conger, whom he subsequently married, as the Bradfords' houseguest.

It was very cold, and when I came in, Mary Rose said, "Lyle, the most horrible thing has happened. I have just received news that Richard was stricken with appendicitis, and I am taking a plane in half an hour. Will you please stay and take over?"

"Yes, of course," I said. "Who is coming to dinner?"

"Nobody but you and Marge Hunter, and of course Gwyn and John."

Gwyn had not yet come downstairs, and Steinbeck had not yet arrived at the house. We sat in the library with its book-lined walls, while Joe Gilmore maneuvered drinks for us from Louise and Lucile, put coals on the fire, and generally stirred around in the room adjusting things. Mary Rose left for the airport, and soon Marge Hunter came in carrying a little muff. She sat down in an armchair on the side of the fireplace, and we began to talk. A little later Steinbeck arrived and Miss Conger came downstairs. A beautiful girl, all in blue, she reclined upon the sofa and said, "Lord, I'm tired."

Steinbeck, a very tall man, stood leaning with one arm on the mantel above the fireplace. Joe put on more coal and shook down the ashes. Treadaway seemed to be a little quieted by this. I wanted him to feel at home and to enjoy the people; but the conversation stopped and I found it hard to get it started again. Marge Hunter, always considerate, tried to help, and she said to me, "Why have you never brought Treadaway to see me? You had to wait until some celebrities came before you brought him down."

Whereupon Gwyn spoke from the sofa and said, "Well, of course, Lyle always was an old bastard."

Joe Gilmore burst out laughing and retired to the kitchen. Treadaway laughed, slapped his knee, and said: "Here I come to meet the greatest writer in America, and the first word I hear is 'bastard.' I might just as well have stayed with the boys at the corner saloon."

CHAPTER III

Joe at the French Market

I have already spoken of the fact that Joe was called "Black Saxon."

Now the Lord knows I have never thought of myself as imperious. I am a simple soul and usually accept things as they come, but it seems that Joe had not only built himself up to imitate my tone of voice and my mannerisms, but also had added a great deal of straight Joe Gilmore to the Saxon.

Well I remember the day Carleton King and his sixteen-year-old daughter, Grace, came to the house. Carleton had an old Ford of '38 vintage, which Grace was learning to drive, making patterns of unidentifiable designs on the fenders.

They came into the house on Madison Street, whooping with laughter. Carleton said, "I wish you could see Joe at the French Market; he is positively regal. He makes the Emperor Jones look like a little boy. He goes from stall to stall, where apparently he is on more or less friendly terms with everyone, and says, imperiously, 'This is for the boss, and the boss ain't goin' to take no second-grade things.' "

This was all very interesting to me, because I had never had any previous reports of Joe's emperor-like behavior. Carleton continued, "Joe stopped at the butcher's and said, 'Now I want a good steak.' The butcher said, 'I ain't got no good steak today; come back Tuesday.' Joe said, 'What time Tuesday?' And the butcher said, 'About eight o'clock.' Joe got indignant, and said, 'Man, I ain't got no time to come back here at eight o'clock no day. I'se sleepin' at eight o'clock, and then I has to be busy with the boss. Does I gets the steak, or does I just sits here and waits?' "

"And," Carleton said, "with that, the butcher produced the steak. I joined Joe from my position in the background, and we went on with our marketing. Joe selected grapefruit, tangerines, eggplants, and tomatoes. He sampled each and every one of them, as they were put into his market basket and said, 'if these ain't good, I'll bring 'em back.' "

Then Carleton said to me, "I'm sure that neither you nor I would have the temerity to make such demands on people in the markets; if we did, they would probably slap us down; but not Joe. He defeats them all, and they run around and pull things out from under the counters and from behind screens. You can be sure, Lyle, that Joe gets the best that the French Market has to offer."

I was sitting in the courtyard that day waiting for Joe to prepare lunch, so I asked Mr. King and Grace if they would stay and eat with me. When they accepted, I went into the house to stir up a cocktail. This was, of course, Joe's job, but he was still bargaining at the market.

Foolishly, I had given him twenty dollars, and I knew

[15]

he would spend every penny of it before he got back; but we would have an ice box filled to overflowing, of which he would eat much more than I would. But it did not matter; it was so peaceful and quiet there; I wanted to stay on, with Joe to take care of me, and dream the rest of my life away, while I listened to the chiming of the Cathedral clock.

We had just got settled, decorously drinking, when the courtyard door swung open and in came Joe, accompanied by Edward Tomlinson, an old friend. Tomlinson is a commentator on the radio and does a great deal on the Blue Network concerning Central and South America. He goes frequently from New York or Washington to Guatemala, Mexico, or Buenos Aires, and sometimes he stops in New Orleans to spend a day with me. We called him "the Commentator."

Joe was jubilant. "Look what I found at the French Market!"

I was not sure whether he meant Mr. Tomlinson or the two pineapples and the chickens he was carrying in his hands. He had put the bulging market basket on the floor. I did not even ask him for any change from the twenty dollars. I knew Joe had spent it all.

He stood there, grinning, surrounded by the fruits of his labor at the market, and always desiring to entertain, he said, "Tell the Commentator and Mr. King and Miss Grace that pretty poem about chickens that you and Mr. Eddie made up."

"Tell them yourself," I said. "You know it as well as I do."

And so, holding the pineapples in one hand, and the gutted chickens in the other, he recited:

Very few hens have died in bed,
True, true,
Very true.
Most of the hens I ever knew
Ended their lives in a chicken stew,
Or were fricasseed,
Or baked,
Or fried;
But all of them died. Yes, all of them died.

And none of them died a natural death,
With children watching their dying breath
And standing around to honor the dead.
Yes, very few hens have died in bed.

The same is true
Of roosters too.

"I think I am staying for lunch," said Tomlinson.

"That's fine," Joe said. "I'll make you a drink and stuff you an eggplant with swimps, but as we is all one family here today, and if you don't mind, I'm goin' to take off my shoes because my feets hurts." And so he did.

We sat in the courtyard and drank Ramos gin fizzes which Joe had prepared—a beautiful, cool, creamy drink, ideal for warm weather. As we drank, I was able to give the only apt quotation that I ever made in my life. It is from Kipling, and here it is:

> The sins ye do
> By two and two
> Ye pay for one by
> And the God you took
> From a printed book,
> Be with you, Tomlinson.

Laughing, Tomlinson said, 'This is the best gin fizz I ever tasted; how do you make it?"

And I, remembering that I taught Joe how to make it, said, "Well, I'll tell you," and I began to count off the ingredients; but as I counted them off, I realized I had forgotten one. I could not think what it was, so I called to Joe.

He came, barefooted and carrying the enormous cocktail shaker in his hand. He poured out the dividends in our glasses.

"You remember I taught you how to make a gin fizz?"

"Yassuh."

"Well, I have forgotten one of the ingredients," and I named to him the ones I remembered.

He stood grinning at me. I said, "Tell Mr. Tomlinson what it is; I've forgotten."

And Joe said, "Nosuh, Boss; if you is forgotten, that is all the better for me, and I ain't goin' to tell you, Suh, because the making of drinks is a strictly confidential secret."

CHAPTER IV

Aunt Patsy, Robina, and the Flower Pots

It was sometime in midsummer when I realized that I must get away for a few days of rest if I were to continue with the job I was doing.

So Joe and I set off in a car for Melrose Plantation—near Natchitoches, Louisiana. I have a little house at Melrose on the Henry Plantation—a charming little eighteenth century cottage of cypress timbers and adobe. It is very simple— four rooms, all in a row, opening north and south, with a twelve-foot brick-paved gallery on each side. Some little way off, the house appears large, but when one actually enters, one finds that at least half of the roof covers these galleries.

Inside it is all white-painted paneling with open fire-places of brick, painted white. In the sitting-room the walls are lined from floor to ceiling with book shelves, and it is here that I keep my most prized volumes. Here also is my collection of pre-Civil War Portraits of Negroes. One of these days I hope to give them to some museum or gallery where they will be preserved as Americana.

The other large room is a bedroom, in which there is a four-post bed with a tester. In winter, the bed is surrounded by heavy curtains to keep out the draft. It is all primitive, but I like it.

Now it has always amused me to hear people say: "Oh, how I know you enjoy the serenity and quiet of the old plantation." No more absurd words were ever said, for I have never known a plantation when it was peaceful and quiet. As a matter of fact, it is more exciting than any life I have ever known in the city; for on the plantation there are ten or twelve white persons, and perhaps two hundred Negroes, and in this little community there is constant excitement—love, hate, heart burnings, and joy.

When we arrived at night, we parked the car in the flower garden and went into the cottage. It was July. Magnolias and jasmine were blooming, and the air was heavy with the mingled scents of summer.

Shortly after Joe had lighted the lamps in the cottage, Fugaboo arrived. He is a dimunitive Negro man, now the proud father of three; but I have known him since he was a little boy when he used to drive my old T-Model Ford. Fugaboo announced that Aunt Patsy was dying. So with Joe Gilmore and Fugaboo, I walked through the cotton fields toward the light that glimmered in her cabin. The corn was high around the house; it was growing right up to the porch and the windows; and beyond the corn, the cotton fields stretched out to infinity, it seemed. There was really no place for children to play.

Aunt Patsy was lying in bed surrounded by her children

and grandchildren. The cabin was lighted with one smoking kerosene lamp. She was wearing a white nightgown and her head was tied in a white cloth.

She was very old and black and withered, and she was making a great to-do about going to join her Jesus. Bud, her son, was the father of "seventeen head of children," which he always said were born in "three layers," meaning he had had three wives. Most of these were gathered around Aunt Patsy. She was giving them her last blessing; it was a most impressive sight. Her arms were in the air, and her remarks were being made to God in a most familiar fashión.

It was only then that I realized that Fugaboo was drunk and that he had a pistol in his belt. Here we were—Saxon, Joe Gilmore, and Aunt Patsy, and about twenty-five or thirty assorted Negroes in a little cabin in the middle of a corn patch.

There was a portable phonograph in the room, and Fugaboo wound it up and put on a record. It was something about "This is the story of Sammy Brown, who ate his breakfast and lay back down."

Interrupted in the middle of her harangue to the Almighty, Aunt Patsy was furious, and she raised herself in bed and said, "Fugaboo, you is a heath'n. Why you play that machine when I'se dyin'? I don't want my prayers to be interrupt with them dirty songs." And with that, she stretched out one thin, black arm and stopped the phonograph.

Fugaboo, insulted, pulled the pistol from his belt and fired one shot straight into the air, upon which almost every Negro in the house disappeared. Where they went, I don't know, but they were gone. Only Fugaboo, Joe Gilmore, and I remained.

Aunt Patsy, ninety years old, black and skinny, had dived straight out the window into the corn patch.

Joe and I took the pistol from Fugaboo, admonished him, and took him away.

The Negroes came back one after another—all except Aunt Patsy. She had disappeared into the sea of corn. She did not return until nine-o'clock the next morning and she came back furious with Fugaboo who had disturbed her death agonies.

She lived ten years after that.

Robina Denholme was a great friend of Aunt Cammie Henry (the mistress of Melrose Plantation). We were very pleased, therefore, when we heard the news that Robina was coming for the week end. We all loved Robina and, in addition to that, she and Aunt Cammie were rivals in weaving. Each of them had looms; and of all the foolishness I have ever heard in my life, the talk about the "warp" and the "woof," while the shuttles flew back and forth and they worked at the old authentic patterns they set up, took, as we say at Melrose, "the rag off the bush." One pattern was "Honeysuckle," one was "Going to Texas," and there were a dozen more. I can't even remember the names of them, but it was very funny as Aunt Cammie and Robina discussed them while a Negro man laced up the looms.

Aunt Cammie and Robina began a contest to see which of them could weave a perfect yard; I was to provide a present for the one who made a perfect yard—without one mistake—first. That was one Sunday; the next Sunday

SAXON'S CABIN ON MELROSE PLANTATION – *near Natchitoches. La.*

Robina was to return to spend the week end with us, and she and Aunt Cammie were to continue their contest. It was on this trip too that Robina was to bring with her three hundred and fifty flower pots. Aunt Cammie was attempting some strange hybridization with flowers—something to do with Cape jasmines and japonicas.

On the Sunday Robina was to arrive, Aunt Cammie and I heard that Aunt Patsy was starving to death on Little River about five miles back of the plantation. She had "taken herself there" because she was dissatisfied with her son, Bud's, treatment of her "out in front," which means out on Cane River. She was living there with two elderly bachelor Negro men—both at least eighty years old—and her grandson, Warbaby, had come to me and said, "Mr. Saxon, I'se afraid for Aunt Patsy to live out there, because them old men might 'ramage' her."

I simply shrugged this away and said, "I think it is a little late in the day for that, and besides, I am quite sure Aunt Patsy can handle the situation herself."

On this day then, Aunt Cammie and I went to retrieve Aunt Patsy from her retreat on Little River. Simply to get there was difficult; we had to go five miles over almost impassable roads, through creeks and woods and, it seemed to me, bottomless abysses.

Joe was driving.

Finally the car could go no further; Aunt Cammie and I got out and started to walk. Far down on the bank of Little River was a white-washed cabin. We could see it as we stumbled through cotton rows and around the stumps of dead trees. When we arrived a sloppy-looking Negro woman with a baby sitting on her lap, and very, very pregnant, was

on the gallery. She asked, "You looking for Aunt Patsy?"
We said, "Yes."

And, with a gesture of complete indifference, she said,
"In there."

We went into the little white cabin on the bank of Little
River. Old Aunt Patsy was there. As before, she was lying
in bed, dressed in a white nightgown with a white cloth
around her head. Her spinning wheel was in the corner;
her carding combs that she used to card wool were nearby.
Aunt Patsy had her thin arms in the air, and she was crying,
"I'se going to meet my Jesus! I'se going to meet my Jesus!"

"Well, you had better meet him up on Cane River," we
said, "rather than on Little River, because we can at least
feed you from day to day."

"How am I going to get there?" said Aunt Patsy.

And we said, "We will send a wagon and bring you this
afternoon. Get ready. Get your spinning wheel and your
combs and the rest of the things you have. We will bring
you out to the front again where you can be fed properly
and not starve to death as you are doing here."

Then she said, "Yassuh; would you bring Warbaby with
you?"

So Aunt Cammie and Joe and I went back to Cane River
and procured a wagon and mules, and sent them back five
miles to pick up Aunt Patsy and bring her back to "the
front." Her son, Bud, had a bed for her, and his wife would
take care of her. Aunt Cammie would feed her. We hoped
that her last days would be spent pleasantly.

Now at Melrose it is impossible to do anything simply.
Everything becomes colossally important. To send a wagon

for Aunt Patsy became a major project. At last we got the wagon, however, and two mules, with Warbaby to drive them back to Little River. We said we would meet them on the way back.

We had forgotten about Robina. Strange things had happened to her on her way down from Shreveport to Melrose. When Aunt Cammie and I reached the plantation, Robina had arrived. Always composed and calm, this time she astonished us by being rather white around the mouth and faintly perspiring.

We said, "What's the matter?"

And she said, "The most horrible thing happened. I had the back of the car full of flower pots packed in straw, and as I drove from Shreveport, I felt so well and happy I lighted a cigarette.

Gaily I thought, "A good week end."

Robina continued, "Then I threw the cigarette away, but unfortunately a draft caught it and brought it back to the car. The straw caught on fire. Everything was burning. My new car! I didn't know what to do. I pulled up on the side of the road and got out and began to throw the flower pots out of the car on the ground. Someone stopped and tried to help me—a nice man; I wonder who he was. We put out the fire in my car, and there I was with all these flower pots, and the road all on fire, because the dead grass had caught too. I had to drive the car away until the nice man could retrieve the flower pots and put them back in the car. It was really the most horrible experience, but here they are—the flower pots. Only a few broken, and I can get some more."

Aunt Cammie said, "Robina, we have to get Aunt Patsy.

She is coming back from Little River—five miles away. Do you think you can drive your car?"

"Of course," Robina answered. "Let's drive as far as we can and meet her."

On the edge of the field we met Aunt Patsy's entourage. It seems that every Negro in the place had decided to enjoy the expedition. Aunt Patsy was lying on a mattress, and the Negroes were sitting all around her. Aunt Patsy, fanning herself with a palmetto fan, dressed in white as usual, with the white rag around her hair, was complete mistress of the situation.

We turned about and accompanied the wagon and the Negroes to Bud Williams' cabin. And so we went back to Melrose, rather tired, rather worn out, on a Sunday afternoon of so-called "peace and quiet" on the plantation.

As we drove into the flower garden at Melrose, some tourists arrived. They wanted to look over the place and see the "quaint" old plantation of which they had heard so much. What we really wanted to do was to go inside and have supper, but the tourists were merciless. They wanted to see this and that, and that and this, and we allowed them to do so before going into the big house.

One of the tourists reached a high point of fantasy when she said, "You know, I saw the most remarkable thing up the road. There was a woman trying to sell flower pots. She had parked there and in order to attract attention, she had set fire to the grass. Everything was blazing, and she was offering flower pots for sale."

Whereupon Robina screamed three times and pretended to faint.

Aunt Cammie and I said, "Stop it!" And she did.

CHAPTER V

Massaline and Murder Gumbo

Massaline was black and fat. She was also married to a man named "Puny." Why he had such a name it was difficult to understand, as he and Massaline were married when she was fourteen and, at twenty-one, she had seven children. Puny, despite his name, must have been, I think, pretty good.

Massaline also had a sense of humor; and she played a game. She used to come over to the cottage and bring me a cup of coffee, and "borrow" fifty cents day after day after day.

All of the Negroes were very interested because they could not understand why I lived alone in the cottage far away from civilization. I had heard comments.

Sammy Peace said, "I can't understand it. He ain't hiding out from the law, 'cause he has people coming to see him."

"I can't understand it neither," Puny would say. "I don't know. He sits here all day long and plays with that little type-writin' machine, and people sends him money through the mail."

Massaline, a satisfied wife, was also curious. She kept asking me questions.

"What you do to make your living?"

"I write books," I said. "Not very good books, but books."

She looked at the shelves of books against the wall, and said, "Did you write all them?"

"No," I replied, "I have written only four books so far, and I don't have any of them here. Some day I'll show them to you."

"Thank you, Suh; could you lend me fifty cents?"

Saturday came, and in the mail I received a letter from a library in New Orleans, saying they were sending copies of each of my books which they wished autographed. Massaline brought me the package from the commissary and post office, and also a cup of coffee, for which I received the usual request for fifty cents.

I opened the package and showed the four books to Massaline.

"Look, Massaline, you have been asking me what I do. I write books, as I told you. Here they are; for the first time you can see exactly what I have done. First, here is *Father Mississippi*. It has to do with floods from the Mississippi River. It took me a year to write this. It has a steamboat on the cover and a catfish on the spine. The second book is called *Fabulous New Orleans* and that also took me a year to write. It is illustrated by a very famous illustrator. That is why it will probably sell a little from time to time. The next one is called *Old Louisiana,* and while I can't think you would be very much interested, it is about old plantation life prior to the Civil War. This last book is called *Lafitte, the Pirate*: it is a biography. Now Massaline, you have seen all the books I have written—one, two, three, four. You understand, this is what it has taken me four years to do. You have seen me at the cottage all these years punching at that machine."

Massaline, sweet and concerned, turned to me and said, "Oh, Mr. Saxon, I don't know, I don't know. You work all them years writing them books and here they is. You ain't sold never one of 'em."

And I said, "Well, give me back my fifty cents. I need it."

"Nosuh," she said, "but I'll go back and make you some red beans and rice. You needs that." And she went back with Joe Gilmore and made the red beans and rice and by God, I liked it.

There was another time at Melrose when Joe and I were visiting. It was again midsummer, and I was sleeping under a mosquito *baire* in the old four-post bed. Doors and windows stood open, mosquitos droned, and from Cane River came the incessant chorus of bullfrogs.

Joe was sitting in the doorway half-naked and half-asleep, waiting, I suppose, for some rendezvous of which I was unaware.

I was lying on my back with a candle in a flat candle holder on my chest, a Bible held open, and I was reading *Ecclesiastes*. Don't ask me why. Perhaps I was disenchanted that night.

Suddenly, through the night, there came a shot. Now at Melrose one doesn't shoot indiscriminately, and I realized that something bad had happened. "Joe," I said, "get me shoes and a bathrobe. I've got to find out what this is."

But I did not have to find it out, for J. H. Henry, Aunt

Cammie's son, the manager of the plantation, came in and said, "Lyle, something bad has happened. I need you."

"Yes, of course; but what?" I answered.

He said, "You know Sammy Peace's wife, Mattie, left him and was living with a colored man down at Cloutierville; but she decided she was tired of that love-life and she wanted to come back to Sammy. So she did; and then this colored man came from Cloutierville to Sammy Peace's house and said, 'I wants Mattie.'"

J. H. continued: "I was asleep; my wife and I were on a sleeping porch and Sammy Peace came and stood just outside the screen-wire and said, 'Mr. Henry, that man is trying to get my wife. What must I do?'"

"And I said to Sammy, 'kill the bastard.' Of course, I didn't realize what I was doing, because as I said, I was still half asleep, and about ten minutes later I heard a shot. It woke me."

Just then Sammy Peace came outside the gallery and said, "I shot him, Mr. Henry, and he is daid."

J. H. said, "Oh, God, he used my pistol; it's gone."

And Sammy said, "Here it is; I gives it back to you."

The rest was a nightmare. Negroes came from all directions, carrying lanterns and flashlights. J. H. telephoned the town fifteen miles away, and asked the sheriff and the coroner to come as murder had been done. There we stood all night long with the dead Negro right at our feet between the house and the kitchen near the little gallery.

Mattie, Sammy's wife, who had hidden herself up in the rafters, was screaming. J. H. and I had to call her down.

We said, "For God's sake, stop that screeching!"

Mattie quieted down, and asked, "Does I make your coffee?"

"Yes," we answered; and so order was preserved.

Morning came; the relatives of the dead man drove up in an old car. By this time the sheriff and the coroner had also arrived and gave us permission to have the body taken away. So they tied the dead man on the running-board of the car. He was stiff and they could not get him inside. Day was breaking; the sun was rising, and the cotton fields were white with blossom when the small car with the dead Negro was driven away.

Sammy Peace was arrested and taken to the town of Natchitoches. All of us were tired and worn out with the murder. We went back to bed.

Aunt Cammie came to my cabin the next afternoon and asked, "What has happened to Sammy Peace? He hasn't brought the coffee this afternoon."

And I said, "Why surely you know, Aunt Cammie; Sammy Peace killed a man last night for fooling with his wife, Mattie."

And Aunt Cammie said, "This is perfectly ridiculous; he killed that man defending his own home and his wife." And with that she went to the telephone, called up the sheriff, and said, "Sheriff, this is Cammie Henry. You have my man, Sammy Peace, in jail for killing another Negro; he did it in the protection of his own home and his wife, and I will sign any kind of bail or bond, but I want him back here, because I want my coffee."

Sammy Peace returned the next day; coffee was passed at five o'clock, in the morning, at six o'clock, at seven o'clock, at ten o'clock, and at four in the afternoon.

Life resumed its even way. We had forgotten the murder; we had forgotten this violent existence. Life was smooth and temporarily quiet again, and we were happy.

Only Massaline was worried—I have never known whether she was named for Nero's mother-in-law, whose name was *Messalina,* or whether Massaline was a corruption of the French name *Marceline*—but she was worried over the Sammy Peace murder. She came to me and said, "Don't you hear them dogs howl all night long? Sammy Peace is in plenty trouble. Sammy Peace has done commit murder."

By this time I was tired of the whole business. I said, "Massaline, I have put up with all of this as long as I can. I don't care whether murder has been committed or not. I am worn out with it. Sammy Peace killed that man protecting that wife of his and his own home. It was murder that was justified, if any murder is ever justified, and why are you making all this fuss about a simple little thing like one man shooting another man? It's been done before."

Massaline turned and said, "It is all right to kill a man if you wants to; but Mr. Saxon, if you is going to kill a man, you don't ask him in the house to eat and give him a plate of gumbo and then shoot him like Sammy Peace did."

CHAPTER VI

Concerning Wigs

Joe and I arrived late another night at Melrose and went to my little house. The next morning, being tired, I slept until noon. He finally got me dressed, and we walked over to the big house for lunch.

Victoria, good, big, and black, stood in the kitchen doorway and said to me, "Oh, if I'd know'd you was here for lunch, I'd have choked another chicken."

Victoria was one of the most colorful figures at Melrose. Her chief characteristic was that she was so good. She had adopted two children—Crooks and Puny—and had raised them to manhood. Her story about it was short, simple: "Their pa was a bad man and he fell out with his wife. They was living in a little cabin on the riverbank, and he come home one night and she wouldn't let him in because he had been drinking and he was violent. There was a little hole in the door where a chain went through with a padlock —you knows how that is; and when she wouldn't let him in, he got mad and borrowed a shotgun, put the shotgun through the hole in the door, and shot her and killed her.

There was them two poor little babies and I took 'em in and here they is. I calls him 'Crooks' because he's got a club foot. Puny married Massaline. Now you got the whole story."

Joe was standing beside me, listening. He was pleased with Victoria. She was so friendly and honest. I left him in the kitchen with her when I went into the dining-room for lunch.

When we had finished eating and the white folks had dispersed to their various occupations, Joe and I went back to my little house, and he said to me, "Miss Victoria needs a wig bad."

I said, "Wig?"

And he said, "Yes. She won't talk to you about this like she talked to me, but she is nappy-headed. She ain't got no hair at all and she keeps her head tied up in a rag. She said if you ever wants to give her a present, bring her a wig, because that is what she wants most of all."

And so I did.

On the next trip to Melrose, I brought Victoria a wig. I bought it on Dryades Street in New Orleans from a hair store. There are two kinds of wigs for sale there. One kind is sort of stationary, you might say; it is combed and fixed in place, and all you do is put it on. They cost $6.50. Then there is another type with hair that can be let down. They cost $10.50. It was the more expensive type I brought to Victoria, because I liked her so much.

She was tremendously proud of this wig. In fact, it became the talk of the plantation. Her friend, Clemance, envied it. Victoria was constantly taking down her hair and putting it up again, even as she fried chicken or baked bis-

cuits. She had had it only two days when a calamity oc-
cured. While she stooped over to put wood on the fire, a
spark flew out, and set the wig on fire. Such screams! Such
lamentations! But she managed to extinguish the flame; and
there she stood holding the precious wig in one hand, and
her nappy head exposed to the public view.

The damage was small, however, and the wig was soon
restored, slightly charred. Many times since, I have seen
Victoria with a gardenia in her hair, walking along the road
in the evening as she went home from work.

Joe continued to be pleased with Victoria. He liked her
because she liked her wig. For some reason, he did not like
Clemance. He said to me, "If Miss Victoria ain't careful,
Clemance is going to steal that wig."

It seems, however, that Clemance had had a wig of her
own. Finally the story came out, as things do in the country
in Louisiana. One listens, and one learns.

Clemance's wig had also been the talk of the countryside,
but unfortunately, she had had a slight affair with a Negro
preacher. One night her husband, Manuel Hunter, was
absent, and the preacher was with Clemance in her cabin,
sitting beside the fire. As I heard it, they were roasting
sweet potatoes in the ashes, and Clemance was being seductive. Manuel arrived earlier than she expected him,
hitched his horse to the post by the gallery, and came in.

Overcome with jealousy at the sight of Clemance and the
preacher, he did the most dreadful thing one can do. He
grabbed her wig off her head and threw it in the fire; and
there sat Clemance, nappy-headed! This may not sound
like an international episode to you, but on the plantation,
it almost caused a revolution.

Clemance came in the next morning with her head tied up in a *tignon,* and said, "I've thrown Manuel Hunter out of the house. I'll have no more to do with that man. He done burnt my wig."

Mrs. Henry, the owner of the plantation, trying to console Clemance, said, "What can I do?"

Clemance said, "Me, I got to get me another wig." And so Mrs. Henry loaned her money and ordered another wig from Sears Roebuck, in Dallas, Texas. When the wig arrived, we all admired it. Clemance was restored to her former dignity. However, in some manner, the second wig also disappeared, and Clemance envied Victoria.

One night as Joe and I sat beside the fire, someone came shouting outside and said, "Miss Victoria done fell out of the porch swing on her head. Could you get a doctor?"

Now at Melrose it is extremely difficult to get a doctor. We are fifteen miles from Natchitoches and it takes hours to get a doctor over there, or from Cloutierville, the town on the other side of Cane River.

Joe helped me get into shoes and an overcoat and we started down the road to Victoria's house. It was too late; there was no need for a doctor. Victoria was dead.

She had taken the day off and had made herself a large dinner of mustard greens and pork; and being fat, and probably ill—although we did not know it—this enormous amount of food had been too much. Her children said she had been sitting on the swing trying to breathe, and suddenly pitched out of it on her head. (She was wearing the wig.)

When I arrived at her house, the children were all crying. Victoria was dead; there was no question of that.

She had belonged to some sort of burial society and they sent from Natchitoches to Melrose, picked her up, and probably embalmed her. She was returned in a coffin she would have admired a great deal if she had been alive. It had a great, silvered plate on top, which read: "At rest."

At the plantation house, we were all sorry about Victoria; she had been so good and we liked her so much. Also, she had been an excellent cook. And now she was gone.

Mrs. Henry and I went to the funeral, which was on a Sunday afternoon. We were the only white people there. In a little Negro church on the riverbank, Mrs. Henry said to me. "I wish we could open that coffin. I would like to look at Victoria once more. I am sure Clemance has stolen her wig."

CHAPTER VII

Zeline

Across Cane River from my house at Melrose, about half a mile away, lives Zeline—a light mulatto—and her husband, Joe Rocque, who would be a replica of General Beauregard if General Beauregard had been badly sunburned. Zeline is ninety years old and she owns one of the little houses that line the river. Hers was a part of the old Convent of 1820. Both the house and the Convent were built of enormous cypress logs, unpainted, with a filler of mud and moss which is like adobe. Inside Zeline's house is painted light blue; the floors have worn out long since, so most of them are earth.

There were always kittens asleep around the fireplace, almost buried in the ashes in the wintertime, and I have always wondered how they escaped the cooking pot.

"What's that you are cooking, Zeline," I used to ask. "Don't tell me you are cooking kittens in that iron kettle on the fireplace."

"No, Mr. Lyle," Zeline would answer. "We don't cook cats yet, but we might some day."

The yard, shaded by china-ball trees, is filled with the

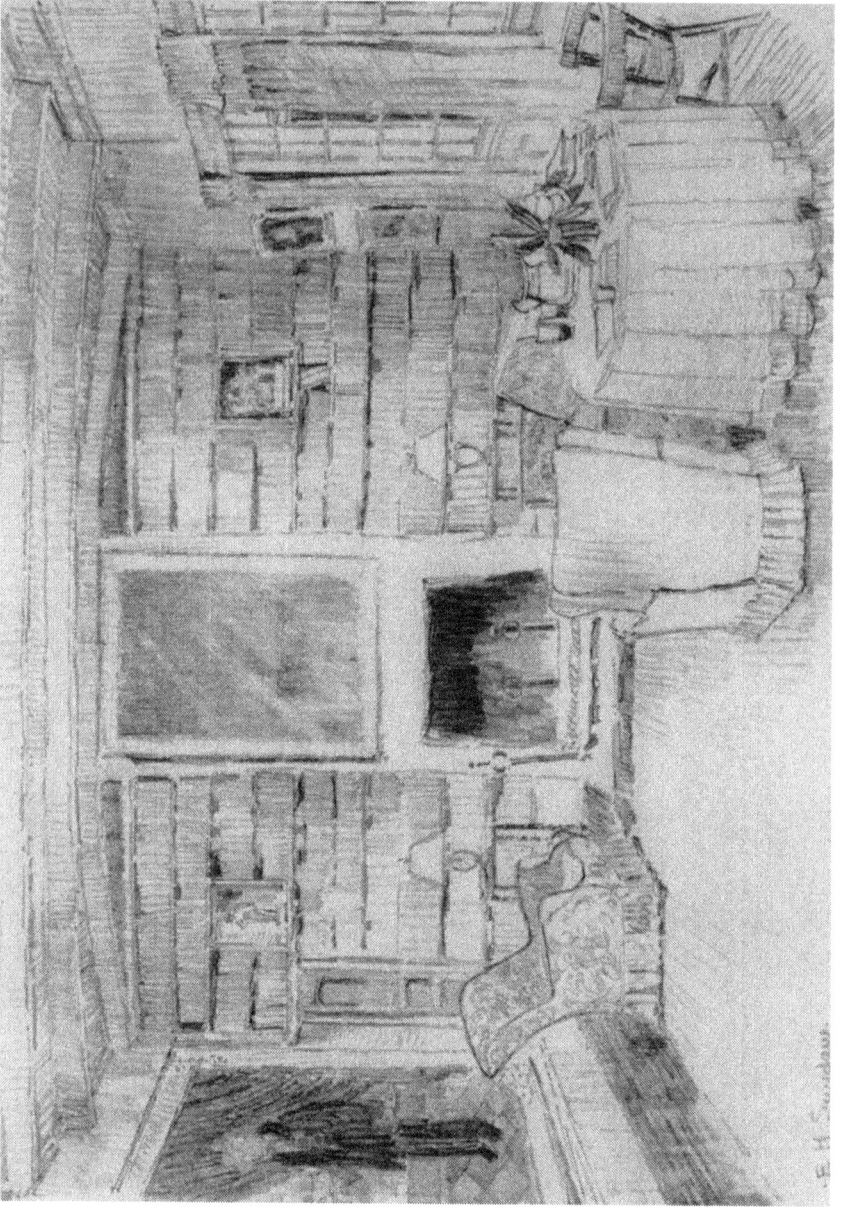

INTERIOR OF SAXON'S CABIN — *Melrose Plantation*

most peculiar looking animals. Zeline's dogs are a curiosity; they are light yellow, with pale blue eyes, and they all smile. Walking about the yard, it is almost impossible not to step on the chickens and dogs. Zeline does not like any chicken unless it is frizzled; many of the turkeys run about on webbed feet, half of the chickens have the heads and necks of turkeys, and there is one particular rooster which looks like nothing I've ever seen before.

In the afternoons, Joe Gilmore and I would sometimes walk across the bridge over the river to spend a quiet and happy hour with Zeline. For, although she has never been more than twenty miles away from the place where she was born, she is a woman of the world. "I am six years older than Joe," she would brag, "but he ain't never looked at another woman since he knowed me."

I used to sit beside her on the gallery on her little house, and we would talk about old times on Cane River. One winter day she told me a story I have never forgotten and never will.

She said: "Mr. Lyle, you don't know what it means to be ninety years old and have your husband eighty-four. He has rheumatism; the house is old; the fire goes out, and we lie up in bed and can't sleep; and I feel sorry, sorry for poor Rocque. We used to have such a good time together, but we can't do that no more. Just the other night I had been asleep and waked up, and I knew Rocque was awake. I stuck my elbow in his belly and said, 'Is you sleep?' and he said, 'No, Zeline, I ain't sleep. These pains keep me awake; and I don't know what to do because everything hurts me so.'

"And Mr. Lyle, I thought hard about it and I wanted to

[39]

tell him something that would make him feel better, but I could not think. But I thought and thought, and I finally remembers we had such a good time together when we were young. I wanted to say something to cheer him up, and I said, 'Rocque, tomorrow when we feels better, and when we is on our feet together, I tell you what we going to do; we going to breed that old yellow rooster to a duck!' "

CHAPTER VIII

Weeks Hall

That old plantation house in New Iberia, "The Shadows," is one of the most beautiful dwellings in Louisiana. The house is set deep in a three-acre flower garden behind moss-draped live oaks and tall hedges of bamboo. It is built of warm, rose-colored bricks with eight large, white Doric columns across its façade and a blue slate roof broken by dormer windows. The house is rich and beautiful in detail.

The garden is divided into three sections. A semi-circular walk leads to the front door. It curves again to the gate. On the east end of the house is a formal garden with high clipped hedges and many magnificent camelia bushes. Some of them are as old as the house. This garden has a brick-paved walk, a fountain, and a magnificent old sundial; at the four corners stand Greek statues representing the seasons. It is mellow and charming.

Behind the house is a side lawn with a summer house at the end; beyond that lies beautiful Bayou Teche—blue by day and silver by night—and beyond the bayou is a thickly wooded terrain, also part of the original property.

The house is set flush with the ground. The rear façade is beautifully austere. There is no veranda but three double white wooden doors are set close together opening into a loggia paved with brick and white marble. This gallery gives access to the sitting-rooms in front, to the dining-room and kitchen on one side, and to the servants' quarters on the other side. In one corner a staircase rises to the second floor, supplementing the stairs on the front gallery.

At one end of the second story there are large double parlors, connected by sliding doors, which open on one side into the garden before the house. Four other windows open along the side to the west of the garden, while windows to the rear overlook the bayou.

The woodwork is carved with acanthus leaves with dainty rosettes at the corners. The mantlepieces are black marble. The parlors may be reached from the upper floor gallery which is serviced by the outside staircase, or may be entered from the rear through a square hall which corresponds to the loggia below. This hall has several windows which look out to the lawn, summerhouse, and bayou.

The guest rooms are all furnished in true plantation style with huge four-post beds and other antique furniture. Family portraits look down from the walls—walls which are faintly grey. The woodwork is white. Beyond the guest rooms on the east side of the house is a master bedroom which overlooks the flower garden. Another flight of stairs rises to the third floor which is surprisingly large. One half of it is divided into bedrooms and the remaining half is the attic. Here, thirty-five or forty leather trunks hold the old costumes and relics of the family. Everything is there, including suits of blue and Attakapas cottonade homespun so popular with plantation owners in the eighteen-thirties. Old armories are filled with papers and account books of the plantation. Chests of drawers are packed with old letters and diaries. Everything is intact—the house, furniture, ornaments—just as it was one hundred years ago.

The Shadows was built by David Weeks in 1830. It is now the property of his great grandson, Weeks Hall, one of the best artists of Louisiana, a bachelor, and a man with an amazing sense of humor.

He is the last of his family, just as I am the last of mine, and we have known each other since we were boys through many years of laughter and vicissitudes. Due to a blood transfusion between us at some past time we now consider ourselves related and when he writes to me—and what letters—he usually begins "Dear Cousin."

Joe Gilmore knew Mr. Hall in New Orleans, where he visits frequently, and Joe was extremely curious to see The Shadows.

"How come you don't take me to this house?" he said, as he sat looking at a photograph of The Shadows. "Who takes care of Mr. Weeks? Is there a place for me to stay?"

"That's a good idea, Joe," I said. "I have been wanting to go over there for a long time. I think we will go and pay Mr. Hall a visit, whether we will be welcome or not. And I think that you and Mose will like each other."

"Who's Mose?" Joe wanted to know, already suspicious, as he always is whenever I mention the name of a colored person he doesn't know.

"Oh, he works for Mr. Weeks just as you work for me," I said. "His name is Emperor Mose, but somehow Mr. Weeks can't bring himself to call him 'Emperor.'"

"Is he a ladies' man?" asked Joe.

"I am afraid so," I said, "and I have a suspicion that if we do go visit in New Iberia, you and Mose will disappear and Mr. Hall and I will be left to wait on ourselves."

Joe was highly pleased with this idea and said immediately, "Now you know perfectly well, Boss, that I never leaves you. I is with you night and day."

"A likely story," I said. And Joe retired to fix me a drink.

"When does we leave?" he said as he closed the door.

And so I telephoned to Weeks to say we were coming.

"You couldn't have picked a better time," he said. "There will be a full moon by Sunday." So Joe and I set out in a battered car for a visit.

The drive from New Orleans to New Iberia is a beautiful one. The road runs west into the Bayou country of Louisiana—a country of sugar-cane fields and sugar houses, a country filled with Negroes who till the land. At intervals one passes a white columned plantation house, at the end of a long avenue of moss-draped trees, drowsing towards dissolution.

The road curves beside curving bayous, and like all curving roads, it offers a constant challenge to the imagination. This is the Acadian country; the land of sturdy French farming people—people who have kept their traditions for more than one hundred and fifty years, and still speak French. There are many Negroes who do not speak English but who use a French patois which, it seems to me, contains many nouns but few verbs.

The road passes through typical Southwest Louisiana towns—Houma, Morgan City, Franklin, into New Iberia, where The Shadows stands hidden from the highway behind its unclipped bamboo hedges—thirty or more feet high.

As we turned into the gate, Joe's remark was characteristic: "It looks just like its picture only it is bigger than you said it was." He was looking about fascinated by the columns, and the oak trees, and the general feeling of elegance and ease.

As we approached the house we came face to face with a statue representing Spring—a female, clad in scanty Greek robes, holding a large garland of flowers. I will never forget how he looked when he saw the statue, his black face, blacker still against the background of the white pillars of the plantation house.

Our host came out the front door to greet us. He had a mint julep in his hand which he gave to me as he called back over his shoulder,

"Oh, Mose, here's our company."

Mose and Joe Gilmore stood and looked at each other, at first suspiciously and then—who can say what signal passed between them?—they broke into wide smiles and shook hands.

"Well," I said to Weeks, "I see that our visit is going to be a success." And so we sat there on the broad gallery sipping our juleps while Joe and Mose brought in the bags. We could hear them laughing together in the kitchen.

After dinner we strolled out to the summer house overlooking the bayou, and some of Weeks' friends came in to call. The moon was nearly full and the bayou was filled with shining ripples. Great trees arched over our heads where we sat in the shadow. There were a number of us just sitting there, lazily enjoying the magnificent night. Joe and Mose in their white coats made spots of light in the shadows as they went back and forth from the pavilion to the house with their trays of brandy or highballs.

It was a magic night, and Weeks had prepared entertainment for us. I saw him smiling as he lighted his pipe and I knew some surprise could be expected. It was not long after that we heard the tinkle of a mandolin and a guitar, and the sweet notes of a violin. The wall of bamboo parted and three Negro men emerged carrying their musical instruments.

Weeks called them to him and told me their names. They were 'Papa,' 'Kadink,' and 'Tar Boy.' They sat crosslegged on the ground and played for us, disdaining the chairs which Mose and Joe offered them.

It was on that night I heard some of their "sinful" songs for the first time. There was an exceedingly funny one called "Terrible Operation Blues," in which one of the singers imitated a frightened Negro woman singing from the operating table while the doctor performed his terrible operation. In a few minutes we were all laughing at the absurd story the singers unfolded. There were other songs such as "Big-legged Mama Keep Your Damper Down." As a matter of fact it was perhaps a good thing that the songs were close to earth, for with the spreading moss-draped trees, the summer house in the moonlight, the slow-moving bayou which reflected the moon, the whispering bamboos and the rustling canes, it was almost too beautiful—like the second sweet liqueur after dinner.

A song had just ended when Joe emerged from the house and came running across the moonlit lawn. "Boss," he cried, "who you think just come? It's Mr. Suydam. He done followed us here from New Orleans." And sure enough there was Eddie Suydam, all smiles. He had just arrived from New York to make illustrations for my forthcoming book.

As I look back upon that evening, it seems nearly perfect. The women in their white dresses, the men in white linen, the couples drifting in and out. Everything was pleasant and easy, and I think of Suydam sitting crosslegged on the ground beside the musicians, his hand cupped to his ear as he tried to understand the words and the innuendos of some of their songs.

It was a night that seemed to bubble like champagne. No one, it seems to me, said anything particularly brilliant, but we all liked each other and were amused and pleased, and satisfied to sit there and sip cold drinks while the moon moved west in the sky. How far away it seems as I look back upon it, and yet I know that the house still stands there and the moon still reflects itself in the slow moving bayou. Most of the people are scattered and I do not even know where half of them who were there that night have gone or even if they are still on earth. Suydam, poor fellow, died the following year at the height of his successful career. But it is good to know that the house and the trees are still there, and that Weeks still sits in the summer house on summer evenings.

Joe and I had so many amusing things happen at The Shadows that it is hard to choose one episode of which to write. But I think perhaps this story of a winter night will suffice. It is but one episode among hundreds.

It was bitterly cold and drafts stirred the brocade curtains around the bed. These old plantation houses are intended for summer. Cold weather, as cold is counted in Louisiana, is always unexpected, no matter how large the woodpile may be. I had been with Weeks for several days, and we had been going to neighboring plantations while I made notes and Suydam made pencil sketches of the houses and such details of the houses that interested him. These pictures later became illustrations for *Old Louisiana,* but the published pictures constitute no more than half the drawings he made.

It was cold, as I have said, and we returned late one night from a visit which had taken longer than we had anticipated. Weeks, Suydam, and I walked through the cold garden and let ourselves in by the big door of the downstairs sitting-room. The room was in darkness except for a few embers on the hearth from the fire which had burned out.

"I wonder where Mose is," said Weeks.

"And I wonder where Joe is," I said.

Suydam laughed as he answered with another question. "Why ask when you know perfectly well where they are and what they're doing? They're out—what is the phrase they use? *ramblin' and pleasurin' themselves.* Joe gave me that explanation many times."

"In that case," said Weeks, "we will have to forage around and find something to eat or drink.

It was so cold we thought of something hot, perhaps a Tom and Jerry; but Weeks had loftier ideas.

"My granduncle taught me how to prepare mulled wine, and I think that would be an excellent idea for a nightcap." So Suydam and I built up the log fire in the sitting-room while Weeks gathered the necessary implements. Before long a pot was steaming on the coals and we had pulled armchairs from the table around the hearth. Slowly the huge room was warming up and we took off our overcoats and threw them upon the sofa.

"How I dread those cold bedrooms," Suydam said.

Weeks and I began to laugh. "Listen to the Yankee," we said. "Here he is—a cosmopolitan, with a New York-Boston-Philadelphia background, and he is fussing about cold weather in Louisiana."

Weeks went to the window, pushed aside the curtains and looked at a thermometer which hung just outside the glass. "It is only 34°," he said, "not freezing. It seems colder, though."

"That thermometer is a liar," said Suydam. "It feels like zero to me. That's the trouble with your Louisiana weather. The heat melts you in summer, and your marrow freezes in winter."

"Which goes on to explain," said Weeks, "why Lyle and I live here and why you visit us at every opportunity and stay so long."

Suydam laughed. "You win," he said, "but just the same I do wish you would get along with your old hot wine or whatever it is."

As the mixture bubbled in the pot and the aroma of spices filled the room I could hardly wait; and we sat there, the old wine mugs in our hands, waiting for our host to ladle out the drink. What he said of mulled wine was true enough. It warmed the cockles of the heart, whatever the cockles may be. It also warmed our stomachs and our hands, and it was so good that we asked for more—and still more.

I think we were all a little unsteady when we finally put our mugs down on the mantel, banked the ashes, and retired to our respective rooms.

Although fires had been lighted in all the bedrooms, they had burned out and it was still chilly. I undressed rapidly, drew back the curtains, and climbed into my huge four-poster bed. A candle burned beside me, and the blue moonlight poured in through the long windows. Across the room the ashes glowed, and I could just discern the old portrait which hung over the mantel. The bed was warm and comfortable as I lay back among highly-piled pillows, blankets tucked up to my chin.

Above my head the silk tester was like a tent supported by four posts. The candlelight was reflected in the highly-polished posts of the bed, but beyond, the room was in shadows.

I put out my hand and took the old leather-bound book which lay on the night-table. Ten minutes later I was lost in the sad and frightening facts the book disclosed. It was *A Guide to Matrimony*, published in the 1840's, and it was filled with astonishing misinformation. After having read a few pages, I did not wonder that the Creole girls, "those innocent lamps, those dear doves" of our great grandfathers' days were terrified by the idea of matrimony when such a book fell into their hands. I had skipped readily through the courtship and had only glanced at the chapter called "Popping the Question" on my way to the wedding night. Imagine my disappointment when I found it to be only a description of the things necessary in the bridal chamber, such as fresh flowers and champagne, a box of bonbons, and other fribbleries. The practical things—if memory serves—had been forgotten altogether, or had been considered too indelicate to be included; but I could not help smiling as I thought of my Creole bridegroom with all the luxuries and none of the necessities for the wedding night.

"Sorry there are no towels, dear, have a chocolate"; or "There seems to be no water; how about a little champagne?" And so I flipped the pages to a chapter marked "Excesses to be avoided," and here I found a most horrifying suggestion:

> "Little is known of those dreaded maladies sometimes called Social Diseases, but it is noted that these diseases—as dreadful and dire as they are—usually appear more among the profligate and those given to excess than among the virtuous, and those who practice everything with restraint. So it is well to beware of excesses in anything among the newly married."

"Oh, dear Lord," I found myself saying. "Those poor little Creole brides. How this book must have frightened them; the spoiled honeymoon, the tears, the forebodings!" I was amused and sympathetic too, from my position of the comparative safety of a century. I closed the book and put it on the table.

It was at this moment I felt a cold draft and the candle-light flickered. I heard the sound of an opening door, the faint rasping of old hinges. I sat up. "Who's there?" I said. There was no answer, but in the gloom in the far end of the room I could see a white paneled door slowly swinging open. Then I saw the head and shoulders of a horrible old man with huge bulging eyes and protruding teeth. He wore an old-fashioned nightcap, and a robe which appeared grey, and he leaned upon a heavy walking-stick as he emerged inch by inch from behind the door, staring at me with his evil eyes. I could feel the hair prickling at the back of my neck, and my voice was hoarse as I again said, "Who is it? What do you want?" There was no reply and the figure retreated as slowly as he had come, as the door swung to behind him. I was left in the empty room with the pale moonlight shining in the window.

I was sure that Weeks, Suydam, and I were alone in the house; but now what horrible thing was this? I sprang from the bed onto the cold floor, yelling as loudly as I could, "Weeks, for God's sake, Weeks!"

I ran and pulled the door open, but the hall was empty. All doors were closed, and through the curtained windows I could see the summer house standing beside the Teche. There was nobody, nothing—only the terror and me.

I yelled again, even louder this time to my host, and ran down the hall, threw open the door to his room, and bounded in. The room was in darkness, but I scratched a match, yelling again. As my shaking fingers found a lamp, the light spread over the room. I saw Weeks, lying in bed, in a paroxysm of laughter. The nightcap was still upon his head. Grease paint had transformed his face into that of an old man, and the huge bulging eyes were plainly celluloid.

"Of all the damned things," I howled—but a shout interrupted me. Suydam came running barefooted into the hall. "For God's sake, what's the matter," he was calling. I went to the door with a lamp in my hand and at that moment up the stairway, out of the darkness, bounded Joe and Mose, identical in red flannel underwear, and looking for all the world like two devils escaped from Underwoods' Deviled Ham cans.

The rest is anticlimax. Weeks had to do his act all over
again for Suydam. There was much laughter at my expense.
Joe and Mose jumped up and down to keep warm. We
were all wide awake, so we went back into the parlor dragging blankets and in ten minutes were drinking hot Tom
and Jerry's, this time prepared with great rapidity by Mose
and Joe who drank with us—the five of us, three men
wrapped in blankets, and two red devils with black faces
making, I am sure, as ridiculous a group as ever disgraced
an aristocratic plantation house parlor.

CHAPTER IX

Alberta

"Boss," said Joe, "you is just getting crosser and crankier. What you needs is a trip to the country." His wide smile belied the words he said.

"What you mean, Joe, is that you want to go to the country somewhere."

"Boss, I thinks we both needs some air. Why don't we go see Miss Eva Scott? You can stay at the big house and I will stay with Percy Bell and his wife."

This amused me, for I recalled that Percy Bell had a house full of children and I wondered just where Joe would fit in; but the idea of visiting the Scott plantation was pleasant to contemplate.

I have known the Scotts all my life. Their house is one of the most charming in Louisiana. It stands many miles from the highway, in the center of a 3500-acre plantation —a plantation which is no longer cultivated to any great extent. There are acres of virgin forests with oaks and cypresses and many other varieties of lowland trees, and

"BIG HOUSE" – *Melrose Plantation*

on the hillsides grow bays and magnolias. The hilltops are covered with pines, and there are sandy-bottom creeks.

The house was built in 1808, and the Scott family has occupied it ever since. Miss Eva is the last of the line now and lives alone with Negro servants. It is impossible to think of the plantation without Miss Eva, just as it is impossible to think of Miss Eva without the plantation.

I have been a visitor there since childhood and I go at every opportunity, which, unfortunately, isn't often. Joe had driven me there once and had made friends with Percy Bell, one of the mainstays of the plantation. Percy was born on the place and has lived there all his life. He is married and has had—it seems to me—countless children. As a matter of fact, he has had eighteen, and in his whimsical manner named the last child "Seldom." Percy Bell lives in a small cottage not far from the big house. The cottage seems to bulge with children on all sides. Just as one thinks he has seen the last of the family, one or two more appear among the rambling rose vines that cover the house.

I was almost sorry that Joe had mentioned a visit to the Scotts, for immediately I felt the old familiar desire to be back in the country again—a sort of nostalgia for a life I remembered from childhood—a life so good and so peaceful. Nowadays, there are so few pleasant reminders of the past, and the Scott plantation is the one place it seems to me that remains unchanged and unchanging throughout the years.

It was at this moment the telephone rang, and Joe answered. He imitated my voice exactly as he said, "Saxon speaking." there was a pause, and he said, "Is that you Miss

Alberta?" and then dropping into his natural manner of speaking, he said, "Where is you at?" He turned to me. "Miss Kinsey wants to speak to you," he said.

Now Alberta is an old friend. We have known each other for more than twenty-five years. She is an artist who has a delightful house in the French Quarter. It was odd that she should have called at this moment, for she too is a friend of Miss Eva Scott. I took the telephone receiver from Joe.

Miss Kinsey called because she had seen some magnolias blooming and she wondered if I knew where she might get some. She wished to paint flower arrangements.

"That's odd," I said. "Joe and I were just discussing a week end with Miss Eva Scott. Would you like to go too? There must be millions of magnolias out there."

"Why, yes," said Alberta. "I can be ready any time. Shall we go tomorrow?"

"I will send a wire," I said, "to tell Miss Eva we are coming."

Accordingly, the next day, Alberta, Joe, and I started out for "The Shades."

We drove north through fields of young sugar cane. Standing like islands among the fields were sugar houses. It is a placid, peaceful country, and dear to me because it is home.

Alberta had a small diminishing glass through which she surveyed prospects. "I have never painted a sugar house, but I think I shall later in the season," she said.

We drove all day through small towns and a number of plantations, and finally through the cotton country. Thirty-eight miles from the town of Baton Rouge we left the highway, in order to drive four miles of dirt road to our destination. We stopped at a filling station to inquire about the roads. We were told that recent rains had washed out the road that went to the gate of the plantation house and that we would have to take another road which would bring us behind the plantation. As Joe drove through red clay hills and sandy-bottom lanes, Alberta became jubilant.

"I see compositions everywhere," she said, waving her diminishing glass.

This unfamiliar road brought us to the back gate about half a mile from the house, and there among the pine trees was a small Negro church, its bell tower slightly askew and a sign above the door which read: "Second St. Paul's."

"I shall paint that," said Alberta. "Can't you just see it, with the Negros coming out after services—the drab little church, the pine trees, and the bright colored clothes of the congregation? I don't know whether I could sell it, but it is something I want to do for pure pleasure."

"Miss Alberta, I thought you want to paint magnolias," said Joe.

"I do and I shall," said Miss Kinsey, "but I'll paint that church too."

In a few more minutes we were at the house being welcomed by Miss Eva, fourteen dogs, and forty-two cats. Percy Bell was on hand with Marthy, who calls herself Miss Eva's bodyguard.

"I was just thinking about you when I got your message," she said. "Look, Alberta, magnolias everywhere."

So she took Alberta to her room while Joe unpacked my bags in the room downstairs which I usually occupied. Daylight was fading. As I leaned on the window sill, I could see against the western sky a large fig tree in which twenty or thirty turkeys had gone to roost. A few belated chickens straggled by and from the dovecote I could hear the cooing of the pigeons. It was all as I had remembered and, at this moment, it seemed the last link in a chain that held me to the past.

These sentimental reflections were quickly dispersed by Joe's exclamation. "That cat pure scared me," he said, and I looked up to see a large white cat sitting on the bureau. "She looks like a little ghost," he added. The room was growing dim in the twilight, and I laughed to see Joe remove the cat and two others he found sleeping in chairs. "Boss, if we don't put 'em out, they is going to be sitting on your head while you is asleep. And if it is all right with you, I am going back to the kitchen and see what Marthy and Percy Bell is cooking for supper."

Later, as we sat at the supper table, Alberta spoke to Miss Eva about the little Church. "Why that's Second St. Paul's," said Miss Eva. "Where is First St. Paul's?" asked Alberta.

Miss Eva laughed. "There isn't one," she said. "There is a St. Paul's the Second, but there was some disagreement among the members, and they built a rival church which they called Second St. Paul's. They are both standing but the older church is further down the road."

As she paused, we heard Percy Bell, Marthy, and Joe Gilmore giggling in the kitchen. They were listening to our conversation. Joe, always adaptable, was inquiring what the fight was about.

"I bet you," said Joe, "it was because the preacher was

looking after too many of the sisters." Marthy said, "Ain't you shamed, Joe? Folks may act like that in town, but we don't do that out here." Then Percy Bell's deep voice said, "How did you know that, Joe? I tells you about it." But we never heard the story.

Miss Eva said, "Let's go and sit on the front gallery and have our coffee there. The moon will be up soon." And so we sat beside the ivy-trimmed columns of the plantation house drinking coffee in the candlelight.

Marthy appeared out of the dark with the silver pot to refill the cups, and behind her came Joe. I could see his white teeth shining as, without a word, he put brandy into my cup, laid his finger across his lips, and disappeared into the dark. This was done in absolute silence, and I realized that Joe was reverting to country ways and was barefooted.

Neither Miss Eva nor Alberta had witnessed the byplay, nor would it have mattered had they done so, but I was amused by Joe's air of secrecy. When I was quite sure that Marthy and Joe had gone, I said, "Miss Eva, this is the strongest coffee I ever tasted. I am sure it would burn if you were to light a match to it." She and Alberta laughed. "I'll show you," I said, and taking one of the tapers from the candelabra, I touched the edge of my cup. The brandy ignited in a small blue flame.

"You see," I said.

"It's magic," said Alberta.

"It's Joe's magic," said Marthy's voice out of the doorway.

In the morning we were astir early. We had breakfast at one end of the front gallery, the dogs and cats in a pleasant semicircle around us. The air was sweet with the scent of magnolias and Cape jasmines, and a morning-glory vine mingled with the ivy on a nearby column.

"I want to paint that church this morning," said Alberta.

"Do you want me to drive you?" asked Miss Eva.

"No, I would rather walk," said Alberta. "Joe will carry my easel and paint boxes."

"I will come with you," I said, "and see that you are settled, and then I'll come back and wander around and look at things."

"I'll supervise the churning," said Miss Eva. "This is butter day."

So we scattered in various directions—Miss Eva to the back gallery, and Alberta to collect her materials. Dogs and cats went about their usual occupations. Soon Alberta, Joe and I were walking through the checkered sunlight on a path that wandered through a pecan grove. There were persimmon and fig trees as well, and we found ourselves followed by hundreds of chickens, ducks, and white geese which apparently had mistaken the paint box for a bag of cracked corn. A large turkey gobbler barred our way, spreading his wings and dragging his tail on the ground.

"He is really rather frightening," said Miss Kinsey, as I gently pushed him out of the path. "I remember one attacked Mary Rose Bradford at Melrose once, and she ran screaming to her husband for protection."

"One of them knocked me down when I was a little boy," said Joe. "He scared me most to death."

As usual, I was laughing. A great flock of guineas, disturbed by our approach, flew from the tall grass, their raucous cries breaking the morning stillness. "They always sounds like hinges on a rusty gate," said Joe.

We passed from the part shadow of the trees into the open sunlight and skirted the end of the cotton field. In a few minutes we had reached the little church. Joe carried Alberta's paraphernalia to the shade of some pine trees opposite, set up her easel, opened the paint box, and unfolded the camp stool.

"Is there anything else you wants, Miss Kinsey?" Joe asked, but Alberta did not hear him. Already she was studying the possibilities of composition.

Now just here I must say something about Miss Kinsey. When she works, she is so carried away by the subject at hand that she no longer pays the slightest attention to the world around her. Alberta is small, with curly, greying hair, and is very quick on her feet. She was walking back and forth in the sandy loam examining the church at every angle, and soon she was quite oblivious to our presence. I sat down on the steps beside the church door.

"Joe," I said, "I think I will walk down the road about half a mile or so and look about. I have not been back there in years, but if memory serves me I should be able to see the Freeman's plantation from that hill top."

"I didn't know there was another house around here for miles," said Joe.

"The Scotts' cousin lives there; it is a beautiful old house called Hickory Hill. Maybe if Miss Kinsey paints long enough I will walk over to see them. Do you want to come along, Joe?"

"Nosuh," said Joe. "I'll lay down and go to sleep under

one of these trees, and if Miss Kinsey wants anything she can call me."

"She is perfectly safe here," I said, "although this is a lonely road, there is a little house just a bit beyond that turn."

"Yassuh," said Joe, "but you forgets that insane asylum at Jackson is just seven miles from here, and this road leads straight to that place. Suppose one of them crazy people gets out and chases Miss Kinsey?" I began to laugh. "I don't think that happens very often, Joe, but anyway I will take a little walk and be back soon. You stay and have your nap because I can see that is what you want."

"I likes the country," said Joe, collapsing under a pine tree.

So I went swinging up the road looking at the trees and shrubs and trying to identify the various wild flowers. It was so tranquil, and the air was fresh and clean. I could smell the pines. When I reached the hilltop I could see Hickory Hill in the morning sunlight; but it was further away than I had remembered, so I sat down under a tree to consider whether I would walk over or whether I would remain where I was. I closed my eyes. Perhaps I slept.

I was startled by a shout from Joe: "Boss, Boss, come quick; they gonna take Miss Kinsey to the insane asylum!"

I stood up and said, "What are you talking about Joe." He was breathless.

"Boss, I don't know. I hear Miss Kinsey talking to a lady that come riding by in a buggy, and the lady invite her down to her house a little ways down the road for some coffee. I followed her down there and you know, Boss, Miss

Kinsey was sitting on the gallery doing nobody no harm, and I hear that lady go to the telephone and she called up the asylum in Jackson, and she said she had captured a runaway patient and would they send the truck for her."

"But Joe, that's impossible," I said.

"You come with me quick, boss," he said.

So together we went rapidly down the road. As we approached the church, Alberta was nowhere to be seen. Her easel, paints, and camp stool were beside the tree where Joe had put them.

"This way, Boss."

A few moments later, just at the turn of the road, we came upon a small white cottage, and there upon the gallery sat Alberta, placidly rocking, a cup of coffee in her hand. I could see no sign of constraint, but pretty soon the story came out.

The woman who occupied the cottage was totally unfamiliar with the ways of artists and when she had seen Alberta in her gay-colored smock, walking back and forth before the church, she became curious and stopped. Alberta was still using the diminishing glass, observing the church from different angles, when the lady asked her politely what she was doing.

Alberta, only half aroused from her abstraction, replied, "I am going to paint the church."

Now to this lady, painting a church meant but one thing —ladders, large whitewash brushes, and buckets of paint. She thought it odd that such a diminutive person as Alberta should be contemplating the large task of painting a Negro church.

"Why do you want to paint it?" asked the lady.

"But I like to paint churches. I paint a great many," said Alberta.

"What color do you intend to paint it?"

"Why a great many colors," said Alberta, again shading her eyes with her hands. "But I can't decide where to start."

The lady was convinced she had encountered an escaped lunatic. The asylum pays a ten-dollar reward for the capture of a runaway patient. So she said, "Why don't you come and let me give you a cup of coffee before you start to paint the church?" To this Alberta had, without hesitation, cheerfully agreed.

Joe was dozing under a tree nearby and heard only half the conversation; but when Alberta walked down the road, he thought it best to follow. And as he approached the house he realized that something unusual was going on. He heard the jangling of a telephone bell in the back of the house and he listened to the excited call being made.

"Is this the superintendent of the asylum?" she was saying. "Send a truck at once to get an escaped patient. I found her wandering in the road talking incoherently. She was saying something about painting a Negro church." There was a pause, and then the woman continued, "I don't know whether you have a missing patient or not, but there is certainly a crazy woman here this minute on my front gallery. I am keeping her here by giving her coffee. She may be dangerous." And Joe heard the telephone click as the receiver was placed upon the hook. It was then he came running to me.

I went up the steps on the gallery where Alberta sat, blissfully unaware of her approaching fate. The front door of the house was closed but I could hear the patter of footsteps within. Presently a door was opened gingerly, and I recognized the face of a neighbor—a woman whose name I had forgotten, but whom I had met years before.

"I am sorry I can't introduce you, but I don't know your name," said Alberta to her hostess. "This is Mr. Saxon, and we are over visiting Miss Eva Scott."

"Good Heavens," said the woman," visiting Miss Eva?"

"Miss Kinsey is an artist," I said. "She is going to make a painting of the little Negro church."

"Oh, Lord!" said our hostess. "A painting of the church. I thought she said she was going to paint the church. Excuse me just a minute."

She ran back into the house, leaving the doors open behind her, and a moment later we heard her on the telephone again. She gave her name and Joe and I gathered she was speaking to the asylum again.

"I made a terrible mistake. I telephoned about an escaped patient, but that is not right. She is an artist visiting Miss Eva Scott. Stop the truck." A pause. "Oh, thank Heaven they haven't started yet."

She came back to the front gallery. Joe and I could contain ourselves no longer. We were both laughing, and when Alberta heard the explanation, she did not think it funny at all.

"I never heard of such a thing. I don't think I want to paint that old church anyway. I could not find the right composition at all. I think I will go back to the Scotts' house and paint magnolias."

On the way home, Miss Kinsey's sense of humor overcame her indignation, and by the time we reached the plantation house, she was laughing too.

"And the worst of it all," she said, "was that I wanted a second cup of coffee."

Joe said, "I'll go back in the kitchen and get you one."

When Miss Eva heard the story, her laughter was unrestrained, and from the kitchen there came an echo as Joe told the story to Percy Bell and Marthy.

When Joe came with the coffee a few minutes later, his hands were shaking so that I was afraid he would drop the tray, and after we had taken our cups, he stood looking from one to the other and suddenly we were all laughing again.

"Now you know, Boss," he said, "Miss Alberta ain't crazy. I don't see how the lady could make such a mistake, because if she knows Miss Alberta like we does, she knows she ain't insane. Why she never even takes a drop of nothing to drink." And turning to Miss Eva he said, "I suppose you knows Miss Alberta is a *tetotalist?*"

CHAPTER X

Dixie and Mary Collins

Opposite the St. Charles Hotel where I live was Dixie's Bar of Music. Dixie is our local Texas Guinan, and her bar is always amusing. I have known Dixie for ten years or more, ever since she was a clarinetist in an all girls' band and attracted my attention by her vivacity and by her ability to put over a song. In those days she was traveling about; but later she opened a bar of her own. It became a place much frequented by entertainers from other night clubs and its atmosphere is highly informal.

It was through my friendship with Dixie and her sister, Irma, who presides at the cash register, that I managed to get a little way behind the scenes in the nightlife of New Orleans.

Joe of course had been friendly with the bartenders and waiters, and Dixie sometimes calls on him to help out on a busy night.

Her bar is long and semi-circular, and behind it the wall is covered by a large mural painted by Xavier Gonzales. The mural consists of a group of caricatures, with Stokowski conducting a chorus made up of well-known entertainers of our day. Bing Crosby, Kate Smith, Vincent Lopez, Benny Goodman, and the Ink Spots jostle each other in friendly confusion. Mae West and Dorothy Lamour sing seductively. There are perhaps thirty entertainers on the canvas.

The guests who sit at the bar amuse themselves by trying to pick out the celebrities depicted on the wall before them, and it is against this background that Dixie puts on her show.

There is a small piano and a pianist—usually a pretty girl; a man plays the guitar, and another the double bass fiddle. The orchestra varies; sometimes there is a trumpeter, sometimes not. And there is always Dixie and her clarinet. From her point of vantage on the platform, she is able to look over the heads of those at the bar and see the guests seated at the small tables beyond. She has that gift so necessary in conducting a club in that she can do three things at once; she sings, she plays with apparently carefree abandon, and she exchanges jokes with the guests. This is interspersed with sudden shouts: "Vincent, catch Table 17," or "Joe a guest is at the door," or "Look who's here." Nothing escapes her notice.

Joe and I were returning from a jaunt one night and I asked Joe to drive me to Dixie's for a nightcap. It was just before midnight, and I wanted to pay my respects to Dixie. Dixie was singing, but she motioned me to wait, and when she finished she came and spoke to me across the bar.

"Our friend, Miss Mary is a little boxed, and I think you might take her home if you will," she said.

Mary Collins is one of the owners of the Café Lafitte, one

of the most interesting of the French Quarter bars. It is in the old blacksmith shop of Lafitte, the Pirate, and to call it highly picturesque is to make a very mild statement. I have known Mary for years, and there is a joke between us. Sometimes, should my name be mentioned, Mary will tell an acquaintance that I have treated her shamefully:

"He promised me a debut party in 1915. That was the year of the big storm, you know, so my debut was put off. Then World War I came along and we forgot all about it; but as the years rolled along, he kept promising me I could take my rightful place in New Orleans society; but he always forgot, and just when we both got around to remembering it again, World War II came, and my debut has been postponed again. I hate him for making me wait, but he tries to cheer me by saying when the time comes I'll be the oldest living debutante. I hate the man."

A statement of this kind often puzzles tourists, just as some of Mary's other statements have puzzled me. For example, I was sitting with Eddie Dreyer and Bill Glasscock decorously drinking in the 500 Club one night, waiting to hear a new entertainer who was said to be excellent, when the door opened and Mary came in entirely alone, her white hair dishevelled, and her well-tailored coatsuit awry. She was carrying a cane; she walked directly to me as I sat behaving myself and doing no harm to anybody. She pointed her cane at me, and cried out: "And so I took the star sapphires and threw them in the river."

She then burst into tears, turned on her heel and strode out of the Club, slamming the door. When I asked her later for an explanation she said she had entirely forgotten the episode, and would I please mind my own business and not come bothering her with talk about sapphires; she had never liked them anyway.

So when Dixie asked that I take care of Mary, I realized that my task would be a delightful but difficult exploit. There was Mary walking around the tables, loving everybody and telling them so, except for a few whose faces did not appeal to her. As I went over to her, she was speaking to a Marine, who stood six feet four if he stood an inch, and she was saying: "I wish you would go home; you are too big and too unattractive."

Dixie was shouting and singing and apparently paying no attention, but when I walked up to Mary and put my arm around her, Dixie saluted.

Then began an argument which lasted for some time.

"Didn't Mary want to go home?"

"No, Mary didn't."

"Didn't Mary want to come sit down and have a drink with Uncle Lyle?"

"Certainly she didn't."

"Wouldn't Mary like a breath of fresh air?"

"No, Mary thought the idea tiresome."

"Was Mary enjoying herself?"

"She was not; she hated the place and couldn't think why she came there."

"Would Mary like to go across the street to Flynn's and have a drink?"

"Mary thought that might be a good idea."

So Mary and I left Dixie's. Joe was waiting outside in the car.

"Would Mary like to go for a ride?"

"Mary might, but she didn't like my car; she thought it

"MUSHROOM HOUSE" – *Melrose Plantation*

E. H. Suydam

might be better to go riding in a Yellow Cab, or perhaps a Checker—or one of those white things. She thought it might be a good idea too to see the show at the St. Charles Cocktail Lounge."

But after a little more persuasion, Mary finally decided she would take a ride in my car.

"That's right, Miss Mary, you get right in," said Joe, holding open the door.

"None but the rich enjoy life," said Mary settling herself.

Joe got in and started the engine.

"Where do you live?" I asked, for Mary is constantly changing her place of abode. Sometimes she lives in Algiers across the Mississippi River, sometimes in uptown New Orleans on one of the fashionable thoroughfares; but more frequently she lives in the French Quarter.

"How I wish it were Mardi Gras," she said.

"Why?" I asked.

"Then I could wear my traditional beard."

"But it isn't Mardi Gras; it is nearly Easter."

"Can't we go to an Easter egg hunt?"

"Mary, where do you live?"

"Guess."

"Come on, Mary, tell us."

Joe turned from the driver's seat and said, "Come on, Miss Mary, tell the Boss where you lives; we want to see your apartment."

"Why hello Joe, I did not see you."

"Where you live, Miss Mary?"

"Guess."

And so the three of us began a guessing game.

"Is it uptown?"

"No."

"Is it in Algiers?"

"No."

"Is it in the French Quarter?"

"Yes."

Then came the elimination of possibilities.

"Is it one of the cross streets?"

"No."

"Is it one of the streets leading to Canal?"

"Yes."

"Which one?"

"Guess."

"Is it Burgundy?"

"No."

"Is it Dauphine?"

"No."

"Is it Bourbon?"

"No."

"Is it Royal Street?"

Mary sighed. "How did you know?"

"What number, Mary?"

"Guess."

Joe started the car, and I knew he had decided to drive to Esplanade and Royal and start to traverse the twelve squares toward Canal. Somewhere in this vicinity Mary lived. That much we knew now.

As we drove down Bourbon past the night clubs, I tried to question Mary further, but she was now singing the chorus of "Alma, Where Do You Live?" and waving to her friends and acquaintances along the way.

It was almost midnight and the streets were packed with sailors and soldiers and their girls going from café to café and from bar to bar.

When we reached Esplanade and Royal, and the car turned towards Canal, the game began afresh.

"Is it in this block?"

"Certainly not, you know perfectly well I do not live this far away from Café Lafitte."

In the next square I asked again, "Is it here?" But she again answered, "No," vehemently.

And so we progressed until we came to the 900 block. "Is it here?"

Whereupon Mary looked at me and folded her hands under her chin, and said, "How did you know?"

Joe's shoulders were shaking. I could see he was delighted with my plight, but he slowed the car down and began to creep along.

"Is it on the other side of the street?"

"No."

"Well, have we passed it?"

"No."

And then, "Is this it, or this, or this?"

And suddenly she said, "Yes, this is it."

It was the Cornstalk house, famous for its cast-iron fence of cornstalks and morning-glories. Mary and I got out and mounted the steps.

"Have you a key?"

"No."

I tried the door and found it locked.

"Is there a key hidden somewhere?"

"Yes."

We began to search, and Joe finally discovered it under a flower pot.

Once in the hall, I said, "Now, Mary, please tell me where is your room."

There was no reply.

It turned out to be the front room downstairs, just opposite where we were standing. We went in. Mary was feeling fine; she produced a decanter, and we had a nightcap. She was so gay I feared she would go out again, so I began saying, "Mary let me help you to bed."

"Of course not, I do not need any help; besides I want to talk about my debut party."

"Come on Mary, let me help you take off your shoes." But she had kicked them off already. Coatsuit and all, she had piled into bed.

"Mary, you'll go to sleep like that; let me help you off with something."

"I can take care of myself," Mary said. "Is that Joe in the hall? Joe can turn down the bed."

"But you are on it."

"I'll get up."

So Joe turned down the bed, and Mary got in again with all her clothes on.

Suddenly her humor changed, and she began to thank me for seeing her safely home.

"I can't tell you how I appreciate your taking care of me," she said, suddenly bursting into tears. "You are just like a father to me."

Joe began to laugh, but Mary was irritated.

"You wouldn't laugh if you had known my father. Look,

this is his picture, I keep it here in a silver frame right by my bed, and every night I kiss it before I go to sleep."

This proved too much for Joe, and he retired to the hall.

"Now Mary, promise me something. If I go and leave you, you won't go out again, will you?"

She considered this for a moment with heavy eyes.

"I promise if you'll do something for me," she said. My patience was wearing thin. I was worn out.

"What?"

"I want you to kiss my father's picture good night."

"But, Mary, Good Lord. . . ."

"Now look, you would have loved him if you had known him. Now you kiss that picture." She sat there, looking at me belligerently.

And so I kissed the picture.

From beyond the door I heard an explosion of mirth from Joe. I knew I would never hear the end of this. Mary turned over in bed. "Good night, darling," she said.

"Good night, Mary," I said. Joe was waiting. I went out and closed the door.

CHAPTER XI

A Mardi Gras Party

At one time the St. Charles Hotel was noted for the number of permanent guests who lived there. Nowadays, the hotel will not rent to permanent guests any longer, but those who have been there for years have not been disturbed. I am practically a newcomer, having been there only eleven years. But there are others who have lived for thirty or forty years in their suites or rooms. We stay until we die. It is a sort of joke.

Just a few doors away from my room, on the corridor, lives Judith Hyams Douglas. She was a schoolmate of my mother's and I inherited her as a friend. Mrs. Douglas defies human limitations. She is an excellent lawyer and a prominent clubwoman—in fact, she has been a founder of several of New Orleans' leading women's clubs. She is also a very active member of a society which does social work. In addition to this, she is on an almost continuous round of social activities.

In those happy days before Carnival was suspended until after the war, Mrs. Douglas and I would join forces in a Mardi Gras party, lasting all day on Shrove Tuesday. The guests were an odd assortment, young and old, sober and frivolous, all joining on Mardi Gras for a day of pleasure. "Judo" Douglas and I would rent the "grand ballroom," and each of us would invite our own group of friends. The parties were highly informal. The only stipulations were that each guest should be in costume and masked. We would serve a buffet luncheon, as it was almost impossible to jam one's way into any restaurant on Mardi Gras. Sometimes we had a small orchestra, so that those who wished could dance.

Judo's guests were representative of the *crème de la crème* of New Orleans society; mine were writers, painters, newspaper people, and, of course, Joe Gilmore, who presided over the waiters, ordering them about as though it were his party.

"I wants everything to be right," he would say. "Mrs. Douglas and the boss will put up with no triffling. Lemme see if there is enough of that crab-meat salad." As a matter of fact, Joe was in his element on that day. He pretended not to hear comments from the colored waiters and bus boys, such as: "Joe sho' is showin' off today," or "Who he thinks he is?" But there was no real friction, as Joe was liberal with dispensing various beverages to those who were serving the guests.

Some of us were there in costume and masks before ten o'clock in the morning. Others would come in after witnessing the arrival of the Zulu King in the Negro quarter later in the day; still others would drop in as the spirit moved them. Few of them stayed very long—usually only long enough to have a quick cup of coffee or a drink, make some adjustment to a costume, or collapse a few minutes on one of the sofas to gather their strength before going out into the streets to mingle with the throng of maskers.

Such an odd assortment we were, and what good times we had! Our costumes were widely varied—Spanish ladies leaned on the arms of ragged tramps, nuns danced with devils; and one year a group of our friends came as Greek statues, wearing white tights and white wigs, their faces painted beyond recognition with a heavy coat of white grease paint which blotted out eyebrows, eyelashes, and lips. Joe was particularly delighted with these.

The Greek statues had rehearsed carefully, and as they appeared in the doorway of the ballroom, shrieks of laughter greeted them from all directions. While more decorous guests sat sedately upon sofas, in costumes of court ladies and gentlemen, colonial dignitaries, and characters from favorite operas, the statues went into their act. Three of the girls struck the pose of the Three Graces, their diaphanous robes settling about their white tights as they took the poses. Three of the men—one large and rotund gentleman—and two smaller men—carried with them a huge snake made of white oilcloth and stuffed with cotton. Someone played a series of chords on the piano and they all fell into the pose of *Laocöon*. There were numerous other poses—carefully rehearsed but entirely forgotten before the day was over.

At the beginning of one year's party, Joe came and plucked at my elbow. "Who's that?" he said, and in the doorway stood Madame Butterfly, herself, in embroidered, flowing robes, and coal black, highly lacquered hair, with a large paper chrysanthemum over each ear. She wore a half-mask from which depended a ruffle of black lace, disguising her completely.

"I don't know, Joe," I said, "But I will find out."

"Suppose she don't belong in here, and just trying to crash our party? We can't have that," Joe said.

"We'll see," I said. I have forgotten to mention the fact that I was a white rabbit that year—six feet, two inches tall with a skin tight costume of white imitation rabbit fur, a simpering rabbit face, ears two feet long, standing straight up and lined with pink satin, a large bow of pink ribbon tied around my neck, and a small bushy tail.

The guests were laughing as the large white rabbit greeted Madame Butterfly with the conventional Mardi Gras phrase: "You beautiful, thrilling creature, who are you?" Whereupon Madame Butterfly turned her back on the assemblage, and to my pleased amazement, I beheld Mrs. Douglas herself. She had appeared earlier to greet the guests in a court costume of some kind, but in order to baffle them, she had gone up to her room and changed into another. Joe Gilmore let out such a shriek of laughter that I had to caution him to be more careful, or the other guests might suspect Madame Butterfly's identity.

That was the beginning of the day; before noon the room was filled with people. There must have been more than a hundred there—ballet dancers, clowns, and characters from opera and mythology. We even had a mermaid that year who complained that she never realized what her mother must have gone through in the days of hobble skirts. The real New Orleanian, who masks, likes to make himself as ridiculous as possible. The "pretty, pretty" costume is tabu.

One can always tell the true New Orleanian by the absurdity of his makeup on Mardi Gras. Of course there are countless youngsters, most of them of high school age, who like to come in a group all dressed alike, and they usually form gay spots of color in the streets with their identical costumes. But our guests had all long grown tired of the idea of trying to be charming; all we wished to do was to be funny, and I must say we succeeded pretty well that year.

Joe was running about jubilantly, approaching this masker and that and asking the identity of each. He would return to me and say: "You just won't believe it suh; the couple over there are Dr. and Mrs. John McBride; you know they comes to see Mrs. Douglas and they comes to see you sometimes. Didn't you tell me he was head of the English Department at Tulane University?"

I said, "Yes, Joe, how delightful they are."

They were burlesqued as George and Martha Washington, with their costumes a little awry, and later on they indulged in a sort of jazz minuet, with a zebra and a Carmen Miranda making up the set.

"This is the best party we ever had," said Joe. "Boss, who is that lady with the snakes in her hair?" I turned to look, and there behind me stood Medusa—an appalling sight, with a bland, wax mask and a wig made of coiled green snakes. From the coils protruded other smaller snakes that quivered as she moved her head. She wore a green Greek costume, embroidered with silver, and around her neck was a snake so lifelike that at first I believed it to be real. Beside her stood a male figure representing Death—he was wearing a black monk's cowl and robe with a skull face seen through a black lace veil. He carried a beaded funeral wreath with long purple streamers which said "At Rest." Death extended a black gloved hand to meet the rabbit's paw and I realized that this was Eddie Dreyer. Joe was delighted. "Lawd! I can't believe it, Mr. Eddie. You is wonderful, but who is the lady?" Medusa shook her head and the snakes quivered. Joe got behind me and said, "Boss, that can't be Miss Hazel?" But it was, and after mingling with the maskers a few minutes, and indulging in a quick highball and a brief dance, Medusa and Death went skipping off into a world of make-believe.

Someone touched my elbow and I turned to find Madame Butterfly beside me. "Who were those dreadful creatures?" she said. "They quite terrified me." I told her, and she began to laugh. "They always think of something extraordinary," she said. "Didn't they come as Circe and a drunken pig last year?"

"Lawd God," said Joe, listening. "I wonder if Mr. Eddie would give me that scary costume to wear to the Zulu Ball tonight? Boss, I could scare them people to death."

"I don't know, Joe." I said. "He will if he is tired of wearing it, but if he is not tired of it, I will give you the white rabbit, because I am tired of it now. I look too sweetly pretty for one of my size and shape." Joe looked longingly at the door through which Death and Medusa had gone. "Boss, I don't like to hurt your feelings, but I sho rather have that death thing. You looks funny cause you is so fat, but by the time I cut the legs and sleeves off and put it on me, they would just say I was cute. Excuse me, Boss, I got to go back; these people waiting for their food and drink."

[81]

Madame Butterfly had drifted away and I was joined by Salome and a Scottish Chieftain, guests from out of town who were here for their first taste of Mardi Gras.

Someone touched me on the arm and said, "I have a wonderful idea." I looked around and beside me stood a short, fat Negro mammy with a *tignon* and voluminous skirts of red checkered material. She wore a white apron on which was embroidered, "I nursed your children and grandchildren for fifty years, and you ain't paid me a damn cent." Joe left the punch bowl and came over. "Who is you, madam?" he said. Mammy gave birth to a loud guffaw, and said, "Don't you know me, Joe? I am an old friend of yours," and he said, "Is that you, Miss Burdette?" He doubled up with laughter because our friend, Burdette, is one of the most beautiful women in New Orleans. She looks like a magnolia, but today it had been her whim to disguise herself with black makeup and much padding.

"I have a wonderful idea," repeated Burdette. "I have a baby carriage downstairs and a nursing bottle. It is a strong baby carriage. Could I borrow you as a white rabbit to ride in it and I could walk beside you and feed you Bourbon out of the bottle while Joe pushes you? It will only be for a few minutes. I'd like to confound some of my highly social friends as they go into the door of the Boston Club to sit beside the queen on the balcony." Joe demurred. "I can't go like this, Miss Burdette; I ain't got no costume."

"We'll arrange something," she said, turning to me. "What have you got in your room?"

"Well, I have an old werewolf costume upstairs."

"Oh, no," she said. 'We want something simpler. That would be too confusing to the queen and her court if they try to guess what our group represents—unless of course we could pick up a Little Red Riding Hood somewhere."

"I am confused enough already," I said. "But let's go up to my room and see what we can find." Accordingly, a few minutes later we came down with a clown suit and a wig which Joe squirmed into and we left the party for a little while. Burdette was delighted with the senselessness of our fantastic group. We went down a wide stairway which leads from the mezzanine to the lobby of the hotel, and there stood a rather embarrassed gentleman guarding a baby carriage in which a nursing bottle filled with whiskey was lying.

"I've had a horrible time keeping the maskers from stealing this," he said to Burdette. "You said you would be gone only five minutes and you've been gone half an hour."

But Burdette, unperturbed, replied, "Thank you so much, Charles. It was grand of you to wait so patiently; and I still say if you would put on a mask and come with us you would have some fun." Charles just sighed, relinquished the baby buggy, and disappeared into the bar.

There was bedlam in the streets; bands were playing and maskers were dancing. In front of the Boston Club there was hardly room to move. The Queen was sitting high on the balcony looking at her subjects packed in the street below. The ladies of the court—the debutantes of the season —were calling attention to this and that masker. The Negro mammy threw kisses to the queen and waved cheerfully to her, and you could see the queen was discussing with the maids our possible identities.

At this moment, the zebra joined us, thus adding more bewilderment to those trying to guess what our incongruous group represented. A small band was passing—the musicians were all disguised as Arabs—and behind them we got a glimpse of our friends, George and Martha Washington, dancing gayly together, while a group of savages applauded.

A few minutes later, as the crowds pushed us further down the street, we found the Greek statues, rather mussed up by this time, aboard a packed truck upon which they had climbed. Their brief but classic act was being presented to a howling crowd of maskers and some bewildered tourists. Somewhere in their peregrinations, they had picked up a rather stout lady in a smart coatsuit. She was not masked; she was evidently a tourist; but she had fallen into the spirit of the occasion and was adding quite a touch of the *moderne* to our classical friends. She insisted, I recall, on being one of the three Graces, thus making four in all.

The white rabbit had grown tired of the baby carriage and got out. Joe howled in my ear. "How we ever goin' to get this thing back to the hotel?" Black mammy Burdette yelled back, "We don't have to; just give it away."

Accordingly it was presented to a group of maskers who were tremendously pleased, and a girl wearing a costume of chamois skin and a magnificent Indian headdress of multicolored feathers, stood up in the carriage. Maskers on each side supported her while she was wheeled away—one hand shading her eyes, and the other beating a tattoo against her mouth as she whooped "Wah-Wah-Wah-Wah-Wah." We saw her disappear in the crowd.

"Let's try to find our way back to the hotel," said Burdette.

"Yessum," said Joe. "I knows an easy way, and me, I

don't like it up here with nobody but white people. I wish I was on Rampart Street."

We followed Joe through the crowd up Carondelet Street and came into the St. Charles through the service entrance. Burdette and I, causing a brief sensation in the bellhops' locker room, emerged into the main part of the hotel, and there to our surprise and pleasure we found that the lobby, usually so dignified, was crowded with maskers and tourists, who were watching a group of seven acrobats—men in yellow silk tights—flinging themselves about as acrobats are wont to do. We arrived in time for the grand finale. They had built themselves into a pyramid three men tall, with one supporting all the others; then they came tumbling down, turned handsprings and went dancing off. We were delighted to hear an old lady say, "I never saw anything like that in Peoria in all my life."

When we got back to the ballroom there was Joe, all smiles, dispensing salad and sandwiches. There were also many new maskers we had not seen before. Someone cried: "The parade is coming," and we crowded through the windows to the balcony. On the street below, the cry was repeated, over and over again, "Here they come; it's Rex," and again, "The parade, the parade!"

When the parade passed, some of us settled down again for a drink. Some were eating at small tables. Only twenty-five or thirty of the guests were there. The rest were mingling with the crowds.

In the banquet room adjoining our ballroom, there was a smart luncheon party. Waiters were running back and forth, and we could hear the popping of the corks from champagne. The guests were still arriving for this party; some of them made mistakes in the rooms.

Mrs. Douglas' secretary, who was costumed as Miss America, was shooing them out of our door, for they were not masked. One pretty girl I remember said, "But I like the looks of this party better than ours. I think I will go in here," and she waved and threw kisses to us as she was dragged away by her male escort. "I am frustrated," she cried out. "They never let me do what I want to do."

"Poor girl, she needs a psychiatrist," said a fallen angel who was standing at my elbow; but Joe Gilmore, who was passing with a tray of highballs, said in my other ear, "Boss, she don't belong here, do she? I think she had a few too many."

A few minutes later, there was another commotion at the door, and a masker, dressed as a unicorn appeared, leading a stylishly gowned but unmasked woman by the hand. In the other hand, the unicorn waved a copy of *Time*. Madame Butterfly went to the assistance of Miss America.

"We are sorry," she said, "but it is our rule that you cannot come in unless you are in costume and masked.

"But she wanted to be masked," said the unicorn. "She is my friend, and I have invited her."

"But who are you?" said Madame Butterfly.

The unicorn removed its papier mâché head, revealing the face of one of our most amusing friends, Mrs. Joel Lawrence, so well known to all of us for her caprices.

"Her husband's picture is on the front of *Time*," said Joel.

"But she has no mask," said Miss America.

"Well," temporized Madame Butterfly.

"Who is she, Joel?" said the white rabbit.

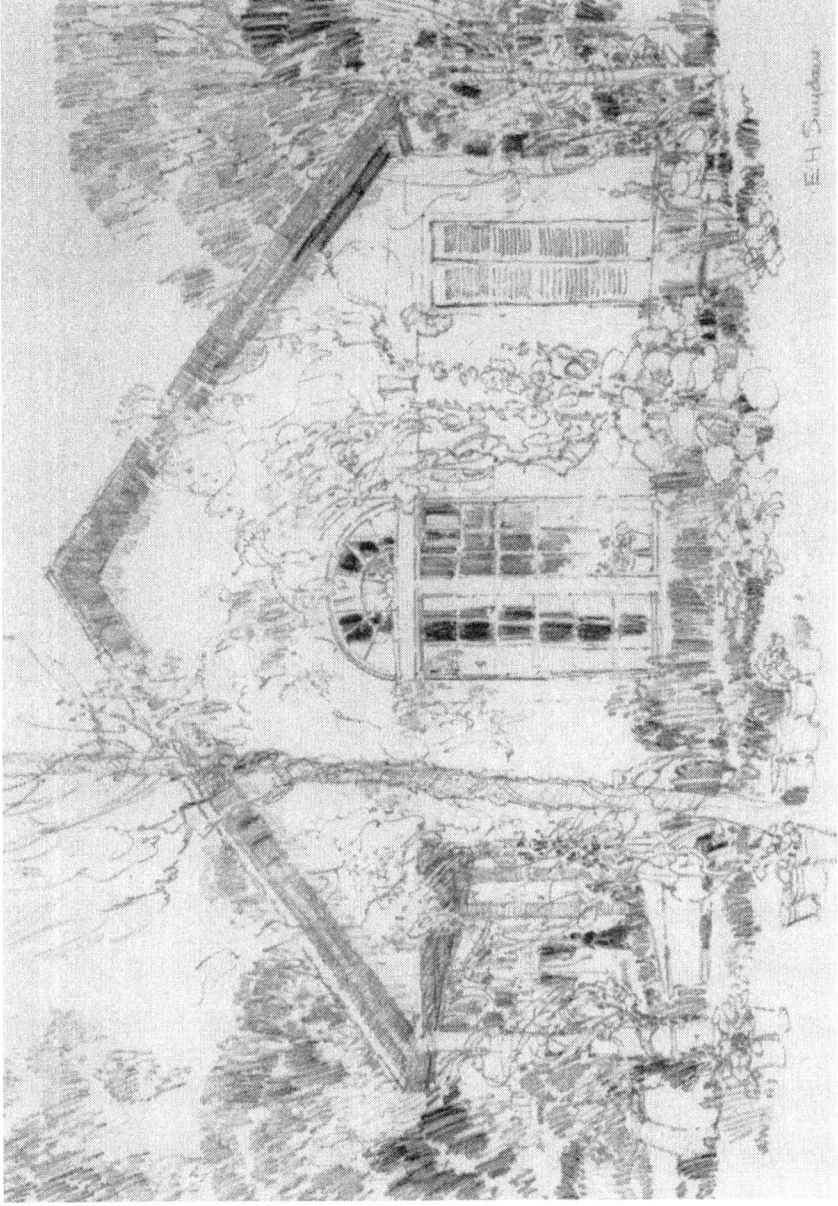

OLD KITCHEN, NOW A GUEST HOUSE — *Melrose Plantation*

"She is Mrs. Donald Nelson," said the unmasked unicorn, "and she is my guest for Mardi Gras."

But Mrs. Nelson's feelings were hurt.

"I've got such a pretty hat," she said, holding it out for examination. "My hat is by Lily Daché, but nobody loves me."

"And your jewels, I presume," said Madame Butterfly, "are by the Baldwin Locomotive Works. Come in and we'll find a costume for you. Joe will take care of everything."

Mrs. Nelson extended her hand and said in her best formal manner, "Till Thursday, then." And in less time than it takes to tell it, she was arrayed in a domino and mask. The Lily Daché hat lay forgotten on a table, as she and Joel and several other maskers took a quick stirrup cup before going out into the streets.

"I wish we had roller skates," said the unicorn.

"This is going to change the whole course of my life," said the domino.

Joe was at my elbow again. "How long is this party goin' to last, Boss? I sho would like to get some rest before I goes to the Zulu Ball."

"It is nearly four o'clock," I said. "We will be finished at five because most of the these people are going on to the Comus Ball, or some other festivity, and they will want to go home and dress."

"What you goin' to do with the rest of the bottles?" said Joe.

"We will save them for next Mardi Gras," I replied.

"Boss, that is the first foolish thing I ever hear you say. Me and them waiters has had our tongues hanging out."

"Well, serve everybody here one last round of drinks,"

[87]

I said, "and then you and the waiters do what you want with the surplus food and drinks."

Joe was laughing. "I'll make the distribution," he said. "I takes what I needs and divides up the rest." The members of the Negro orchestra were picking up their fiddles and guitars before joining Joe and the waiters in a private party behind a screen which concealed a door leading into the service rooms.

There were loud bursts of laughter in the streets below. The crowds were still milling about. Bands were playing, and no one seemed to be tired.

But our party in the ballroom was coming to a close. Masks were removed; we laughed at each other and shook hands and called it a day.

"See you early next Mardi Gras," we said.

We did not know at that time that there would be no "next" Mardi Gras. Instead there was a war.

CHAPTER XII

Joe at the Railroad Station

The war, of course, made many things different. Howard Hunter was leaving the Madison Street house to return to Washington, where he had been called for some kind of conference. Marge Hunter and I were to see him off; she intended to stay a few days, put the apartment in order, pack their clothes, and then join him. Remembering that the redcap situation was acute, we decided to take Joe Gilmore with us to the station in order to handle Mr. Hunter's bags and get them into the drawing room in which he was traveling. We were a little late; dinner had been good and we were gay. Joe was wearing a white serving jacket, a rather dirty one.

Finally we could sit no longer. The numerous suitcases were piled into the Hunter car, and we set off for the railroad station. We found that it was fortunate we had brought Joe, for there was not a redcap in sight, and a number of refugees from Pearl Harbor were pouring into the station. There were mothers with babies and luggage, and no one to help them. There were distrait women who appeared as though they did not know what they were doing. There were hundreds of sailors and soldiers. Joe had given us the tickets and, while we stood by the desk having them checked, he was running around grinning from ear to ear. Just at the time we had finished and were ready to go on the train, he appeared and said, "Anything else I can do?"

"Yes," I said, "go into Drawing Room A, on Car B-31, and pour us out a drink."

We all realized Joe's peculiar faculty for producing something out of nothing, so as we walked down the platform and boarded the train, we were not really surprised to find Joe, in his dirty white coat, with three highballs awaiting us. We sat down and drank. Hunter's wife kissed him, we shook hands, and then Marge and I got off the train. They were shouting "All aboard," but the train was still standing there.

Joe had left us and was somewhere out in that melee, and we knew we must find him because we had to take him back to the Madison Street apartment so he could get rid of the jacket and put on his regular coat. As Marge and I walked down into the mob of people, pushing and shoving, we stopped to look. Sailors were telling their girls goodbye as they got on to the train. Service women were getting aboard. People were crying and laughing and carrying on. We understood it and were sad and glad at the same time.

In all this bewildered confusion, I hunted for Joe. I felt that I knew where I could find him. So we kept close to the long line of Pullman coaches. We passed the Pocahontas, the Robert E. Lee, and the Zachary Taylor, and finally, at the Jubal Early, we found Joe in deep conversation with a

Pullman porter. Marge stood looking at him and said, "I wonder what they are talking about."

I thought about this a minute, remembering Joe's vagaries and eccentricities, and said, "I think I know, and if I can surprise him with a question, we will be able to find out."

Marge was pleased with the idea, and just as they cried "All aboard" for the last time, and the porters were putting their steps into the vestibule, I walked up close to Joe, who was still standing at the Jubal Early, and said, "Joe, I know exactly what you are doing. You are making friends with this pullman porter to get his name and address, and the minute the train pulls out, you are going out and try to make a date with his wife."

Joe, caught completely off guard for once, said, "Nosuh! not this one, but that one," pointing to the next coach.

"O.K.," said Marge, "let's go back to Madison Street and let Joe make us a drink. Les ought to be there."

And Joe said, "When we gets home, I will make you and Miss Leo a Pullman Porter's Wife's Special."

It turned out to be straight Bourbon and ice. Joe had his mind on other things.

CHAPTER XIII

Washington

It was not long before I was in Washington too. Here I lived in a rooming-house. It was a funny little house, very pretty and charming, at 503 18th Street N.W., facing the park, and between the two Interior Buildings. The house was painted white with blue shutters. But once you got inside the place, the charm disappeared. It seemed to have been demolished inside, and put back together with paper board, gunny sacks, and thumb tacks.

Downstairs lived Major Berrien Eaton and his wife with their Chinese Chippendale furniture and oriental rugs. Even though Eaton's doors were closed as I entered the place, I could look through the holes in the partition and see the amusing parties he always gave. Upstairs, I was constantly afraid the floors would give way and I would fall down into their evening's entertainment. The stairs were steep, dark, and narrow, and how I ever navigated them without falling flat on my face, I don't know.

I lived upstairs in the back room; in the front room lived a little girl from the Bronx. We shared the same bathroom; but I have a strange feeling that she had never had the advantages of a bathroom, even of such a one as we were sharing. Never have I seen such an array of underclothes as were constantly strung out in that place. The rooms, God knows, were bad enough; but the little girl did not seem to understand that one slept in a bedroom, bathed in a bathroom, and washed clothes elsewhere. I would go into the bathroom, and there was all that absurd underwear—faded pink rayon pants with runs, sleazy slips with cheap lace, and dozens of stockings, all colors and mismatched. I think she took in washing; no one person could have been possessed of such a lot of nasty looking undergarments.

I remember well the evening I rushed home from my work, late for an appointment. I hurried into the bathroom, and the tub was filled with her clothes. I was furious; I rapped on her door and yelled, "Take your clothes out of the tub. I have to get a bath and shave, and I'm late now!"

She opened the door and looked at me with her cowlike eyes, and said, "Some people are mean to girls!"

My office was around the corner in the Walker Johnson Building, on New York Avenue, just opposite the Octagon House. Although my job was difficult, and I did not do it too well, I had an efficient and charming girl named Margaret Ross for my secretary. I told Margaret about Joe Gilmore. In those days he wrote to me frequently, and Margaret would laugh immoderately when I handed over the letters.

Joe was very busy being Black Saxon at that period. I had turned over to him the entire management of the house with the pink arches on Madison Street. He collected the rents, paid the notes at the bank, deducted his salary, and sent the rest of the income to me—the rest being absolutely nothing. There was always something on which Joe had to spend money. I understood all of this and was amused by it because I had never been able to do much better myself.

Here is a typical letter from Joe Gilmore during that time.

New Orleans, La.
March 2, 1943

Dear Mr. Saxon:

I receive your letter, and was glad to hear from you. The five dollars was gladly appreciated. I threw a party for the school teachers with it, they came that following Sunday.

This is Tuesday morning about 9 o'clock, and it is raining, And the flying ants are flying, And I am bathing them with (Flit). I set all the plants out in the yard for that March rain.

Mrs. Willoughby told me she have sent you the check to Washington, After receiving your letter, The Morgans, said they will pay Friday morning, the Peterson is on the 4 Thursday. So I will pay Homestead (Friday) morning. Now I have bough ½ Gal. of flit, for garden & house use for those flying ants at $1.05 qt. ½ $2.10. Paid Ernest for garbage 3 weeks at $.75 wk $2.25

The Morgan borrowed the sofa Sunday, her mother have arrived. This is a rainney, and sad gloomy day, nothing to drink but (Flit) Plenty company of (Flying Ants).

While moving sofa, found David Nichols, Brown pants Underneath sofa covers.

I am trimming all the plants and trees, preparing for the Blessed Event of April 1.

Everything is in tip top shape on Madison st. It been raining since Monday, all day and Yet raining and so far, What a blessing no leaks.

I think it a great honor for Joe Gilmore, to be Mr Saxon New Orleans Banker and Agent.

Tell all the (Friends of Joe Gilmore, Good luck, looking for them for the (Wedding).

Good luck and Best Wishes. (Your Banker).
Joe Gilmore

[94]

The Washington job made me most miserable; it practically destroyed my mind, broke my health, and put out my eyes. I was so pleased to come back to New Orleans; I wanted to get back where I could be quiet. And there was the old house on Madison Street. The sunlight was blazing on the courtyard, but under the arches it was cool and delightful, and Joe was there to make drinks.

The day I came home, Lawrence Lange, a light mulatto, turned up, job hunting. When I was a child, Lawrence had worked for my grandfather. Lawrence had been kind to me in many ways, and I had many reasons to remember him. He was now getting old and a little deaf. Joe was there at the house, and almost my first words were: "Joe, give me a drink quickly, and make one for you and Lawrence, if you like."

I sat in a wicker chair under those pink arches and drank the mint julep Joe brought to me, while I listened to the conversation between Lawrence and Joe. It was calm and comfortable in the courtyard and my nerves had begun to quiet when I realized that they were beginning to have a quarrel.

Lawrence was trying to impress Joe and was telling him about my childhood. My people were simple people and never lived in the grand manner; but Lawrence had been with my grandfather, and probably through the years had forgotten the actual state of our affluence. He was bragging about the grandeur of my earlier life. It was, as I remembered, on the quiet side. Lawrence said, "I taught Mr. Saxon to ride on a pony. That pony was just as gentle as could be, but Mr. Saxon had trouble sitting on him. So I had to ride with him, and if I didn't go where he wanted to go, he'd raise sand. That was a lovely place, and we enjoyed it."

Joe spoke up, "I bet it wasn't that good, Lange. Mr. Saxon, you want another mint julep?"

I answered, "Yes."

As soon as Joe got back with the drink, Lawrence started again with his bragging. He said, "You don't know what a fine place that was, Joe. We had a fish-pond. We built it ourselves and we had a crocodile in it."

"You had a crocodile in it?" Joe asked.

"Yeah," replied Lawrence. "You know what a crocodile is?"

"Yes," Joe said.

"Well," said Lawrence, with great hauteur, "of course some people calls 'em *alligators*."

Joe said, slowly getting to his feet, "Lange, you is drunk; go home." Whereupon Lawrence was gently pushed through the courtyard gate, and I finished my drink.

CHAPTER XIV

Joe and Lucius Beebe

It was a sport coat that started all the trouble. It was very gay—a bright checked tweed—and why I bought it, I shall never know. But it looked warm and comfortable, and I thought I could wear it in the country. It was like nothing I have ever had in the world; and I repeat, why I bought it I just don't know, except that I probably had young ideas. Joe was always very careful about my attire; he wanted me to look dignified, as became my years, and when he saw the coat, he said, "You shouldn't wear a coat like that. You should wear only plain blues in the winter and white linen in the summer." But he was fascinated with the coat, nevertheless.

"Mr. Saxon," he repeated, "that coat's right bright. It's much too loud for you, and I needs it."

I said, "Nothing doing. That coat will be very warm for me in the country and I intend to keep it. Let me alone."

We had just finished this conversation. I had been ill, and was lying on my bed at the St. Charles Hotel in an old, green bathrobe. I had not shaved, in spite of Joe's admonitions that I should get up and get "straight." He had just told me, as he had told me hundreds of times before, and was to tell me hundreds of times later, "You just don't look dignified in that old bathrobe."

At this minute, Lucius Beebe called from the lobby and said he would like to come up for a while. Mr. Beebe and I had the same illustrator—E. H. Suydam—and although I had never met Beebe, I knew about him. Who doesn't? When he came up to the room, I was still in bed, and Joe was busily engaged in laying out my clothes. There was another person with Mr. Beebe, a friend called Chuck, and Joe seated them around the bed. After we had settled down, I asked Joe to fix us a drink. It was all very gala. Mr. Beebe was asking about various things in New Orleans, while Saxon lay on his bed.

After Joe had prepared the drinks and placed them very formally before us, he retired to the far side of the room. However, I could not help noting that he kept eyeing Mr. Beebe's attire, for which the latter is rather famous. Finally, not being able to restrain himself longer, Joe approached our little circle, pointed to Mr. Beebe's coat (an ultra black and white checked sport coat), and in a stage whisper, clearly audible to everyone in the room, said, "Boss, you just can't get away with a coat like that."

There was a moment of consternation in the room. I felt I could not explain the situation, and that any word I could say would only add catastrophe to confusion.

Joe said, "Does I get your coat?"

And I said, "No, you don't get the coat. Fix us another drink."

The atmosphere cleared somewhat as we drank, but on

Mr. Beebe's return home to New York, he wrote a column in the *Herald-Tribune* in which he described me as living in New Orleans, surrounded by seedy splendor and the services of stylish and snobbish Negro servants.

As I had never had more than one Negro servant at a time, and perhaps a cook, it amused me to think of Joe's multiplying as though he were the sticks of a folding fan.

Eventually, Joe won out and went triumphantly home with the coat. But it was too big for him and he had to have it altered. A few days later he came in and said, "I wants you to go with me down on Decatur Street, because there is two signs I wants you to look at. One of them I don't understand, and the other one is going to make you laugh."

So I went with Joe down Decatur Street.

The first sign "bowled me over." It was a homemade affair, the wording was extraordinary, and the letters were obviously painted by an amateur. The sign said:

"Trainient Trade Solicitude."

This was the sign Joe could not understand. I told him I supposed it had something to do with the Transient Hotel near the French Market.

He led me on a little further until we came to the pressing shop where he had taken the coat. It was a wonderful place. Four Negro men were lying asleep on top of the clothes that had been delivered for pressing, and one poor little Negro was pressing clothes. There was the other sign which Joe particularly wanted me to look at.

"Clothes pressed while you hides."

And we were both laughing and I no longer cared about not having worn that bright checked tweed.

CHAPTER XV

Miss Bessie

Joe and I have a family joke which has to do with a happy death. When things go wrong, one of us will say to the other: "Miss Bessie was right," or perhaps: "I envy Miss Bessie." This is a saying passed between us when we find the company boring or life dull, and the saying is particularly appropriate on a rainy day. Many a time Joe has handed me a cup of coffee as I lay in bed, and then, in his best valet's manner, has gone to the window to draw back the curtains. If rain is spattering on the window sill, he is likely to turn and look back at me with a flash of teeth, and say, "Boss, I bet you feels just like poor Miss Bessie this morning."

Let me tell you the story:

Joe and I once drove to Natchez, Mississippi, to visit an old friend of my mother's; I shall call her Miss Laura, as is the fashion in the South. Miss Laura is both a mother and a grandmother, but her girlhood name persists. I am sure that if I were to see her name upon a tombstone, I would feel that something was wrong if it did not carry this familiar appellation.

It seems to me that all my friends represent the end of something; Miss Laura represented the end of an era, the end of "the good old times" of open-handed hospitality and gracious living.

Miss Laura's fame as a hostess had been proverbial, and even when I knew her, long after the dismal drizzle of poverty had fallen upon her, she was still smiling and gracious, and the old silver soup toureen—blue with that luster that comes to silver only after years of polishing—was none the less lovely because it stood upon fine old damask that had been darned and mended many times.

I like to think of her in the bare dining-room in her house not far from Natchez, Mississippi. With the exception of one bachelor son and one spinster daughter, her children were married and gone. And when I came to stay with her, there were only four at the table—a huge and beautiful table that could seat at least twenty persons without crowding. I suppose it would have been possible to shorten the table, but for some reason, not explained and never questioned, the table remained stretched to its full length—a broad expanse of gleaming mahogany, the four of us clustered at one end and an old majolica pitcher filled with flowers at the other. We dined always by candlelight, with the candles protected from the softly moving air by great glass hurricane shades or *cylindres*—a word we borrowed from the Creoles.

The room was large and bare; the carpets had worn out long since and the brocade curtains lived only in memory. As I remember the dining-room, the green window blinds were half-closed in the summer to keep out the sun, but we ate our noonday meal in the pleasant shadow with

streaks of sunlight on the floor, sunlight broken by the out-
lines of the vines that grew luxuriously around the windows.

The food was simple but delicious; but then everything
seemed simple and sweet to me at this bare but welcoming
house. When I was present, Joe would help Melisse, the
cook; and excellent friends they were. We could hear them
laughing in the kitchen when Joe would assist her in serving.

With his usual acumen he knew that these friends were
"quality" and he was very deferential to their wishes. It
was pleasant to see him taking care of Miss Laura. I remember one day in particular—when she commented upon
the heat and laughed because we were eating hot gumbo
on a blistering summer day and because none of us had the
strength of character to resist this dish—that Joe made one
of his gentlest gestures toward her. I can see her with the
silver ladle poised upon the steaming toureen, and I recall
the kind words of thanks she said to Joe—how I wish I
could remember the exact phrases—when, unasked, he stood
behind her chair and fanned her throughout the meal with
a large palmetto fan. It was a moment and time I shall not
forget—the bachelor son and spinster daughter teasing their
mother because she got all of the attention from both Joe
and from me.

"She has always been like that," said Miss Bella. "All of
the men both white and black liked to wait upon her. Nobody fans me." Whereupon Joe, blithely smiling, said, "I
fans you the next time if you wants me to, but your Mama
is sitting by this dish of hot gumbo." And as the soup had

THE CHURCH ON CANE RIVER — *near Natchitoches*

been served, he removed the toureen to the sideboard, came back and resumed his fanning.

Miss Laura knew hundreds of amusing stories of the countryside and I used to hang upon her words. She told me many kind anecdotes of this one or that one of her old neighbors in the country, most of whom were now lying in the small plantation cemeteries of various estates.

Sometimes a delapidated surrey would be brought out and Miss Laura would take me driving over the Natchez streets and through the side roads, passing the houses at which she had visited as a young girl. The surrey was drawn by two white mules, and Miss Laura used to laugh and say her father would turn in his grave if he could see her riding in this fashion. He had loved fine horses; in the parlor his portrait hung on the wall flanked by two smaller portraits, each one representing a saddle horse held by a small boy in livery. Such small touches of elegance in the house were reflected in the touches of elegance in Miss Laura's reminiscences.

I shall never forget one warm afternoon just before sunset when we drove down the country road behind the plodding mules. Joe was driving, and beside him on the seat was an old black-and-white-spotted setter which had gone along just for the ride. "She deserves a little outing," said Miss Laura. "She has been a good, faithful dog, although she'll never hunt again."

The surrey creaked; the mules' hooves clopped on the hard clay of the hills and moved noiselessly through the sandy bottoms. Sometimes we forded small creeks, and there were places along the road where the trees met overhead, making a long dim tunnel with small spots of sunlight flickering high in the branches.

On this afternoon, as we crossed a small hilltop, a beautiful old house came into sight—a mellow house with eight columns across its façade. Sunlight glinted upon the fanlight over the door. The house, once white, was now faded to a soft gray with the window blinds a washed-out green. Framed in live oak trees and seen through curtains of Spanish moss, it had the unreal quality of an enchanted place. I said something of the kind to Miss Laura, and Joe, on the front seat, turned to say, "Looks like everybody is 'sleep in there." When I looked at Miss Laura, I saw that her face was grave and, when she started to speak, I realized that a story was beginning to unfold itself.

"I never pass this house that I do not feel sad," she said; and then added, "stop here, Joe, I want to look around. We were all very happy here when I was a young girl; and Bessie, just my age, was the only daughter. It seems to me I can still see her when I pass, although she has been dead a long time. She is buried over there. You see that clump of trees? That is the plantation cemetery. Drive a little further, Joe and stop again. That's right, stop here; now look, do you see?" And she gestured with her palmetto fan. "There is the summer house at one end, and there beside it where those vines are growing, there is a pile of . . ." She broke off and sighed. "I don't know whether I should tell you this story or not, because sometimes people do not understand it."

I knew better than to ask any searching question, or even urge that she continue. Stories are not told that way among plantation people and one can only ask questions indirectly.

Miss Laura, after a pause, seemed to make up her mind and she continued: "As I said, it makes me feel sad just to drive by here, because I always think about poor Bessie."

There was another pause, and then came the surprising statement: "She died under an umbrella."

Quickly I repressed a desire to ask an eager question, and after thinking a moment, I said quietly, "What sort of an umbrella, Miss Laura?"

The subterfuge worked. She settled back, and the story began:

"It was a large umbrella of yellow and white, and as I recall it had an Italian's name stamped on it. 'Musso' I think. It was a most ordinary umbrella, but it served its purpose." She sighed again, and went on with her story.

"Do you see that little mound over there by the summer house? Well, that is a pile of shingles. It has been lying there for twenty years, and I suppose they are all rotten now. It does not matter any more.

"You see, that was a proud family, and after all the old people died, Bessie was left with her bachelor son. Bessie and I were the same age, and the son was old enough to be your father. They lived pretty much to themselves and they were very poor. They were sensitive too, for they had always held their heads so high. The old house began to go to pieces and a bad leak developed in Bessie's bedroom. Because she was sick that winter, she was in her room a great deal. I remember going to see her and noticing that the rain had spotted the red silk on the tester of her big four-post bed. She laughed a little bit about it and said that all of the bedrooms were leaking, but that through great good luck

[105]

they had found enough money to buy new shingles. The shingles had been ordered and would arrive any day. They had arranged that a Negro carpenter come and put them on. She was very pleased about it, and we joked a little bit about hard times.

"Well, the shingles arrived and were unloaded and piled up right there by the summer house, and the son, Culpepper—that was a family name on her mother's side—was very pleased that the leaky roof was to be renewed at last. The work was to begin the following day.

"But the most unfortunate thing happened. One of the neighbors, really he was a man without any tact whatever, rode by on his horse, and began to tease Culpepper. 'Well, it is high time you had a new roof,' he said. 'I understand that the water drips right through onto your piano in the parlor.'

"Now I told you that family held their heads high, and Culpepper was furious. He said, 'There is no hurry about repairing the roof. I shall do it when I get damn good and ready, but not before.' And with that he turned to the Negro carpenter and said, 'Don't come tomorrow. I've decided to delay the work until the comments of our impertinent neighbors have stopped.'

"Naturally, his neighbor was furious and never spoke to Culpepper again.

"Well, time passed and the shingles lay there and the roof was not repaired. Culpepper would have none of it. I did not dare speak to him about it, but I felt sorry for Bessie up there in the damp. I don't know how she felt about it, but I think she agreed with him on general principles. It was not the business of anybody to comment on their domestic arrangements.

"My, how it rained that summer! It was the wettest August I ever remember, and every time it rained I kept thinking about poor Bessie. Surely, I thought, Culpepper would have the roof fixed by Thanksgiving. But, All Saints' Day and Thanksgiving passed and the shingles lay there. We laughed a little bit about it at home and joked about it in a friendly fashion; but none of us said anything to Bessie or Culpepper. Christmas came, and I dropped over to take a fruit cake. Culpepper met me upstairs in the hall and said that his mother was really sick. And so I went up. There she was lying in that great bed with big stains on the pillow where the rain had dropped through that morning. The red satin on the top of the bed was soaking wet. I just didn't know what to do. I finally suggested that we get some Negroes in and move the bed, but Culpepper said that one part of the room leaked just as much as any other part. Bessie did not say anything. So I left the cake and went downstairs and talked to Culpepper. We sat in the parlor and I let him have a piece of my mind.

" 'Culpepper,' I said, 'it is none of my business whether you have the roof fixed or not, but Bessie is my girlhood friend, and I love her like a sister, and she is sick. I think you should get a trained nurse right away.'

"He agreed with me and he said that he would attend to it at once.

"I went over that night and stayed with Bessie until the trained nurse could get there. None of us said anything about the roof, but it stopped raining about that time. The nurse came in the next morning, and I declare I never was so glad to see anybody in my life. It was really the most fortunate thing that ever happened, because as it turned out she was one of the Magee girls. They were another plantation family nearby."

Miss Laura paused, and I ventured the question, "And did the nurse make Miss Bessie comfortable?"

"Yes, she did. I never saw such spirit in my life. She talked right sassy to Culpepper. 'This is perfectly ridiculous —you and your pride. My father is just as proud and just as silly as you are, but by the good Lord, sir, if I am to take care of Miss Bessie, I am to have full charge.' Now, nobody had ever talked to Culpepper like that in his life, and he just stood there looking at her. I knew those Magee girls and I knew she would get her way, no matter what he did. To tell the truth, I think he was beginning to feel pretty uncomfortable just through that stiff neck of his.

"Along about four that afternoon it began to rain again, and Sally Magee was furious when the drops began to fall on poor Bessie's bed. It was just at that time that a fruit peddler drove up to the house. And do you know what that girl did? She went right downstairs without a word to Culpepper or anybody and she took Musso's big white and yellow umbrella right off his wagon and carried it inside along with a small bunch of grapes she had bought. She just left Culpepper to settle with the Italian. I don't know what arrangements he made, but he probably paid a good price for that parasol. Well, anyway, Sally Magee carried it upstairs and fastened it up in the top of the four-post bed, changed all the linens, and made her patient as comfortable as she could.

"It was not much use though, because pneumonia had set in; and a few days later the umbrella was not needed any more."

Miss Laura sighed and patted Joe's shoulder with her palmetto fan. "Drive on, Joe."

The wheels creaked and the mules began their plodding walk. In a few minutes the trees had cut off the view of the plantation. The story was finished, I thought, but Miss Laura turned to me and said:

"Well, there is one comfort; Bessie died dry."

CHAPTER XVI

Joe Gilmore Leaves and Returns

Sick I lay in the Baptist Hospital—so ill I did not care whether I lived or died. My few friends were scattered to the four winds and the seven seas. Even Joe had the itching foot, and I well knew that he would soon be on his way. So it was no surprise when he came into my room at the hospital—that dreary room with the green walls—and said: "Mr. Saxon, I got a chance to get a job with the Pullman Company if you will give me a letter of recommendation."

"Of course I will give you a letter of recommendation, Joe," I said. "After all, ten years of long, loyal service means something; and if you are going, you are going. I understand things like that."

So I tried to get the letter written. Time-worn phrases played tag with each other in my brain. "He is good; he is honest; he is my friend; and he is going!" That was a bad moment, because everyone else had gone too. Saxon was to be left alone. But I wrote the letter for Joe, and in time I became better and able to stumble around the room with a cane. My moods were varying—varying in degrees of despondency. I wanted the gay and easy life that we had led, which seemed so hopeless now. I thought, "It doesn't matter; I will go on."

But to a man of fifty odd years, an adjustment is a little harder to make than it used to be.

I thought of the house on Madison Street. It had been a bad house for me. In fact, in my despondency I seemed to associate it with every calamitous phase of my life. What was the use of keeping it at all? I had worked so hard—in the house and out of it—but I had had so much fun too.

Well, all right! And so I sold the house, with the pink arches and the cool courtyard paved with flagstones, and eventually I returned to the room at the St. Charles Hotel where I had lived for eleven years.

But I was still miserably sick, barely able to get around with a walking cane. It was not good. One day a postcard came from far away, saying;

"It's cold and strange here in S. Franciscyo."

Then I knew that perhaps Joe Gilmore would come back again.

Weeks passed and nothing happened. I grew no better; my despondency had reached an acute stage of melancholy. One day as I lay on the bed, devastated, I heard a knock on the door. I sat up, picked up my walking cane, and said, "Who is it?"

The door opened and in came Joe Gilmore—my friend, the man with a hundred teeth.

"Mr. Saxon," Joe said, "don't you want me to fix you a drink?"

"How glad I am to see you again, Joe," I said. "How glad I am to see you again! But what's the matter? Didn't you like the Pullman Company?"

"Yassuh, Boss," Joe said, "but they put me on a troop train, and the people called me 'Nigger' and 'George' and you never called me names like that, Mr. Saxon."

I was overjoyed, but I managed to stay calm and said, "Well, Joe, here we are. There is no more house, no more money, and I am very ill. Where do we go from here?"

Joe answered, "I don't know Boss; it don't matter. But I kinda likes working for you, because I always had a good time and your friends is all so ridiculous."

Some Friends of Lyle Saxon

By

EDWARD DREYER

Preface

If Saxon ever told me who gave the party or who the old lady was, I have forgotten; but she had cornered him on a sofa in order to regale him with the story of her woes. He was doing his best as a sympathetic audience, and the Saxon best was remarkably good. He registered horror, amazement, compassion, and understanding as they were called for and murmured, whenever she stopped for breath, appropriate words of sympathy.

Olive (Mrs. Clifford) Lyons, a woman he greatly admired, watched the Saxon performance, though she could not hear the conversation, with amusement. Then, when he was being particularly articulate in expressing concern over some tragic episode in the old lady's narrative, she passed by and, chucking him under the chin, said: "Tut, tut, tut—he doesn't mean a word of it!"

Saxon always liked to tell this story on himself. He was an excellent storyteller, as everyone who talked with him will agree. He could embroider the most commonplace of incidents until they became delightful—just as he could take the dullest of people and, with an unusual social talent, draw out from them a measure of wit and charm.

I did not meet Saxon until 1935. For eight years thereafter we worked together and saw each other almost every day. He told me, during that time, many stories about himself and the people he had known. I have heard him tell some of them over and over again, varying them, whenever necessary, to suit a special audience.

Here are a few. Everyone who knew him at all well will remember some of these stories. Everyone who knew him five minutes will recall at least one other. They will miss, to be sure, the backdrop of plantation cabin, French Quarter house, or fantastic hotel room before which the stories were originally told. They will also miss the props—four-posted beds, sword canes, absinthe drippers, paintings of Negroes and paintings of centaurs—that always seemed to be on hand. But most of all they will miss the voice and the manner of a skilled raconteur who was also possessed of an extraordinary personal charm.

On some of the occasions I was present; but on others, and on all before 1935, I know only variants of the stories as Saxon himself told them. And for all I know he didn't mean a word of it.

I

Saxon, growing up in the town of Baton Rouge, Louisiana (and on a nearby Mississippi River plantation), was
lucky to have had, from his early childhood through his
college days at Louisiana State University, a friend whose
mind was as agile, quick, and humorous as his own. This
was George Favrot, who died in Paris not long after World
War I. George had the same curiosity about literature and
life that Saxon had, though his only published work, as far
as I have been able to discover, was a short story in the old
Smart Set.

. When Lyle was no more than twelve years old (George
was somewhat younger), they came across an advertise-
ment of a certain matrimonial bureau. From one of the
family photograph albums they took pictures of a young
girl of marriageable age as well as pictures of a young man
and, inventing names and backgrounds to go with the photographs, joined the bureau. Throughout a whole summer
the two boys conducted passionate correspondence with
several lovelorn females and a couple of men anxious to
marry a rich and beautiful girl. Then, one by one, their
letters cooled and the various offers were rejected. One of
the male correspondents, however, refused to be put off
and announced his intention of coming to Baton Rouge to

plead his cause in person. For almost two weeks Lyle and George lived in holy terror; but the swain failed to show, and after a while they forgot all about him.

Both Saxon and Favrot were voracious readers with a taste in literature advanced for their age. They made friends, therefore, with the town librarian, a young lady who helped them get access to volumes that might otherwise have been denied. Although they were reading Ibsen and the Russians and anything else they could lay their hands on, they still, however, retained a youthful pleasure in practical jokes.

The librarian was one of those people on whom nature had played a cruel trick. She had an excellent body; her hair, her eyes, her mouth, and her complexion were quite good. Altogether, she would have been a fine figure of a woman if it had not been for her nose. It was a nose that would have put Cyrano's and Punchinello's to shame; a nose that in this day, with plastic surgery, might have been corrected, but in that day, in a small southern town, could ruin a life. She was pleased enough, therefore, with the company of boys who were hardly more than children.

On one occasion, having saved their allowances, they invited her to a widely-advertised movie, to be followed by a treat at the most popular drugstore in town. They knew that like most women, however pretty or plain, she could not resist primping in public. They in turn could not resist, placing rouge in the powder compartment of her compact which she asked them to carry.

At the end of the movie, before the lights were on, she did what probably every other woman in the audience was

GALLERY OF SAXON'S CABIN — *Melrose Plantation*

doing—she powdered her nose. Then she went gaily on with them to the ice-cream parlor, to be greeted by many of the people who used the library, but greeted with a surprise and hilarity which she was at a loss to account for, until she caught a glimpse of herself in the mirror behind the soda fountain. Bursting into tears, she ran home.

At that moment the whole idea no longer seemed funny to Lyle and George. They offered their apologies and tried to find a way to really make up. Though they were formally forgiven, the warmth had gone out of the friendship; it was not until months later that they succeeded in discovering a means to restore the old relationship.

Mardi Gras was soon to be celebrated and they asked the girl to go with them to New Orleans on that day and mask. She refused again and again, but eventually they prevailed upon her to dress up as a French maid of the typical musical comedy of the period—the maid who used to appear when the curtain first went up, tripping in on high heels, sashaying about with a toy duster, and explaining what could be explained of the plot.

And so on that Mardi Gras day, with an abbreviated and becoming frock that displayed her arms and legs to advantage and a black satin half-mask with a lace fringe that concealed her unfortunate nose, she seemed a very desirable woman. Wherever she went, men for the first time in her life were attentive. And Lyle and George knew that at last they were forgiven.

Miss Minnie ——, because she was the only woman in town who had a glass eye, fascinated both boys. One afternoon she made a round of calls on her most intimate friends distributing bits of jewelry and other personal belongings. Her friends protested, but she explained that she preferred to give away such things while she was still alive and could herself enjoy seeing the people she loved wearing the objects she most treasured.

A few days later Miss Minnie took a walk to the outskirts of the town along the railroad tracks. Selecting a place screened by trees and shrubbery, she waited patiently for the evening train. When it drew near she "put her neck on the track." The engineer said he saw her and did what he could to stop the train, calling out and waving at her to get up. She lifted her head, shook it to indicate that she was going on with her plan, then put it back down. It was severed neatly from her body. Later a note was found stating that for a long time she had been suffering excruciating pain as a result of the loss of her eye and that she did not have the courage nor the strength to go on.

Everyone felt sorry for Miss Minnie, though the sorrow was not unmixed with curiosity. The funeral parlor was crowded with grief-stricken friends but also with others who came primarily to see what kind of a job the undertakers had done. Miss Minnie's eyes were, of course, closed, but it was whispered about that the glass eye had been lost and that it was still some place in the grass on the side of the railroad tracks.

The next day Lyle and George spent hours hunting for the eye. As far as they knew, it was never found; at least they didn't find it.

Saxon always spoke with affection of his maternal grandfather Michael Chambers, who ran the town bookstore in

Baton Rouge, in addition to being the town treasurer, and who ruled the household in which Saxon grew up.

Grandpa lived to be quite old and, in his last years according to Saxon, liked to make up rhymes, mostly satiric, about members of his family. He did this while lying bedridden in the four-poster which he later willed to his grandson. One of Saxon's favorite remarks was: "All I ever inherited were inferior cameos and over-sized four-postered beds."

When Grandpa died he had succeeded in outliving all of his contemporaries except one dear old lady whose own hold on life was then extremely precarious. Before the funeral there was much discussion as to whether or not she should be informed. Some said the shock would be too great for her; others that, since she had known Michael Chambers all her life, she should be told. After endless argument the first faction won, and the old lady was, so everybody thought, kept in ignorance.

When the long Episcopal service finally came to an end, Grandpa was lowered into the Chambers family plot in Magnolia Cemetery. The undertaker's assistants placed the artificial grass blanket over the grave. People were beginning to go home. Only then did someone discover the dear old lady sitting cross-legged on a nearby tombstone, swinging her heels. Several of the women rushed over to her with great concern crying: "Oh, my dear! We tried so hard to keep this dreadful tragedy from you. How did you know?" And the old lady, with the triumphant gaiety for such occasions that sometimes comes with great age said: "Ha! You didn't really expect me to miss old Mike's send-off, did you?"

The other members of the Chambers household were Saxon's mother, Katherine Chambers Saxon, four maiden aunts, and an uncle. Of these Miss Elizabeth, Miss Maud, and Mr. Ralph Chambers survived their nephew.

Saxon had many delightful tales to tell of his mother, especially of childhood visits with her to New Orleans (he once got lost in the maze that long ago was part of the park at West End on Lake Pontchartrain) and of later visits to the French Opera. One story in which he took much pleasure concerned a bathrobe she made for him when he was a very small boy. When she asked him if he had any preference he brought her an illustrated edition of *The Little Lame Prince,* that someone had been reading to him, and pointed to the Prince, resplendent in his coronation robes. Presently the royal Saxon was marching off to bed with a small but adequate train flowing out behind him.

Saxon liked to relate one of his Aunt Lizzie's experiences during Reconstruction times when, as a frightened but fascinated little girl, she watched from behind drawn shutters a torchlight procession of Negroes rioting through the streets of Baton Rouge. Of his Aunt Maud, a favorite story concerned a hat she once brought back from a visit to New York. It was a hat that would have been the envy of all the other young girls in town; but just one hour after she had unpacked it, while the family were sitting down to the noonday meal, their old retriever, long since past his hunting days, came into the dining-room and proudly offered to Grandpa the bird that had been its principal decoration.

Perhaps the Aunt who entered most frequently into his conversation, however, was Aunt Jennie Mae. Whenever, as a child, he came into her room, she invariably began the conversation with: "Lyle, dear, please don't make so much noise." He soon realized that she did this quite mechanically—even when he came in on tiptoe and spoke in a whisper. Years later, whenever there was a lull in the conversation, he was likely to start things going again by saying aloud to himself: "Lyle, dear, please don't make so much noise," and then launching into some Baton Rouge reminiscence. On one occasion, when he inquired about her health, her answer so delighted him that he long afterwards used it to reply to inquiries about *his* health. With a wonderful flight of fancy, Aunt Jennie Mae had said: "My whole left side, dear, feels just like a steamboat!"

Saxon much admired his father's mother, Elizabeth Lyle Saxon, who had been active in the suffragette movement and who was the author of a charming book called: *A Southern Woman's Wartime Reminiscences*. She had a mind considerably advanced beyond that of the average women of her time, especially the average "sheltered" woman of the deep South.

Once, when Saxon was a young man visiting in New Orleans, he was sitting on the porch of his Uncle Walter Saxon's house talking with his grandmother. She suddenly said: "Lyle, do you believe in a personal God?" "No," he said. "Good," she replied. "Now we can go on from there." This part of the conversation was overheard by Uncle Walter's charming wife Lulu, who exclaimed: "Oh, Mother, how can you say such things!" To this mother replied: "It's alright, Lulu, you wouldn't understand anyway. Run along and don't bother your pretty head."

Lulu *was* pretty; she was also petite and altogether

charming and had once been on the stage. She liked Lyle because, among other things, he was so tall. Together they would sometimes make an entrance into her dining-room, Lulu perched on her nephew's shoulder, singing a tune from one of her former successes, and throwing kisses.

Her husband loved her completely and for her built a house in the Victorian-Gothic style of the nineties—all turrets and bay windows, colored glass and nookeries. This was in uptown New Orleans in a neighborhood which was then really country.

Lulu owned a parrot who imitated her voice so well that sometimes neither her husband nor her nephew could distinguish between them. One of the things that the bird, whose name was Polly McCaw, said was: "Come in, come in," whenever it heard a knock. Lulu complained that as a result she had no privacy whatsoever. Another phrase the parrot often repeated was: "Hahaha, you don't say!" in a high drawing-room comedy voice. On occasions when guests were discussing the most serious matters—death, grave illness, or calamitous reversals of fortune—Polly McCaw would sometimes embarrass her mistress by crying out: "Hahaha, you don't say!"

When Lulu died, her husband was broken hearted. Sometime later, while Saxon was visiting him, he confessed that Polly McCaw's imitations of his wife's voice had almost driven him crazy. One day he could stand it no longer and, opening the cage, shooed the reluctant bird out into freedom.

Months after, while Saxon was walking through the zoo in nearby Audubon Park with a friend, he noticed a parrot at the very top of the huge flight cage, but on the outside.

"I wonder," said Saxon, "if that could be Polly McCaw." "Impossible," said his friend. "She's probably been dead long ago. She was much too used to being cared for to fend for herself." "Well, there's one way to find out," said Saxon. Picking up a stick he rapped loudly on one of the iron bars of the cage. "Come in, come in," said the parrot and, just to make sure that there would be no doubt as to her identity, added, "Hahaha, you don't say!"

Saxon did not have much to say about his days at Louisiana State University. He had hoped to go to an Eastern college, but family finances would not permit it. This was a disappointment yet, on the whole, he seems to have had a pretty good time. Also, since the school was in his home town, he kept his old circle of friends, especially Mary Bird, his cousin, George Favrot, and Greta Le Sage. Of his instructors, I remember him speaking with particular affection of at least two—Miss Mercedes Garig, an old and dear friend, and Dr. W. A. Read.

He also talked about a girl, a member of his class, who was always neglected at house parties and other social gatherings. She was not actually stupid nor really plain, but she did give the impression of being both. He and George Favrot decided to see if they could do anything about this. First they invented a nickname for her. Then, in the mornings before classes started, one would say to the other: "Have you heard old Didie's latest?" and would repeat something that was certainly considered witty and amusing by their classmates. Soon everybody was calling the girl by her new name and repeating her bright remarks. It was not long before she began to blossom out, pay more attention to her clothes, and even occasionally say something on her own that was funny. From the class wallflower "Didie" evolved into a reasonably popular girl. It was the old case of "a little kindness and putting her hair in papers" doing wonders.

One thing Saxon did not like about L.S.U. was its military training program. He always said that on the day he finished his training he went home, took off his cadet uniform, and threw it away, hoping he would never have "truck with that kind of nonsense" again.

Saxon also did not fancy Baton Rouge as a place to spend his mature years but was anxious to leave its then small-town atmosphere behind. Some members of his family thought he should settle down and work his way into a position of solid security in the local branch of Standard Oil. He had other ideas. As stopgaps he taught high school briefly in Florida and, in Texas, had something to do with making blueprints for engines.

While in Texas, a friend once took him on a tour of one of the redlight districts. Afterwards he liked to recall an inmate of one house so popular and so much in demand that she was allowed to have a private telephone in her own room. For the time and the place this was considered the last word in bawdy-house elegance. He was also fond of repeating a statement made by the madam of another establishment. Swishing through one of the sitting-rooms, her skirts rustling and her keys jangling, she looked with genteel annoyance at one of her girls who was lolling back in a chair, smoking a cigarette, her feet propped up on a table. Then, raising a carefully penciled eyebrow, the madam threw over her shoulder as she made her exit: "Maribelle, you'll *mar* the mahogony!"

Finally, in New Orleans, Saxon rediscovered the city he really loved and found the job for which he was ideally fitted—reporter, first on *The Item* and then on *The Times-Picayune*.

II

One of Saxon's friends, when he first came to live in New Orleans, was Mrs. Flo Field, author of a New Orleans comedy of manners: *A La Creole*. Mrs. Field sometimes took groups of tourists through the old French Quarter and Saxon occasionally helped out. Their combined imaginations produced more haunted houses, more beautiful brides who had thrown themselves from balconies rather than submit to the indignities of the wedding night of a *mariage de convenance*, and more slaves tortured in attics than the Creoles had been able to produce in two centuries. Perhaps their best invention was "Flo the First," who was real enough to begin with but acquired from them a background that became increasingly glamorous and profitable. One day Saxon was accosted in the Quarter by a bedraggled old woman asking for alms and wailing, at the same time, over the death of her poor dead little baby. Since she was seventy, if she was a day, this puzzled him. He knew that in medical history such things occasionally happened, but he doubted very much that this woman had recently had a child. Perhaps, he thought, it was a pet—a dog, or a cat, or even a canary. Perhaps it was a grown son or daughter whom the poor woman, in her befuddled state, still thought of as a baby. Curious, he pursued the subject. No, she insisted, it was a baby, her own baby, a dear sweet little baby and it was dead, dead in its grave, and she was desolate. Then, growing a little weary of her act, she leered at him and added that it had, of course, died fifty years ago.

Saxon was determined that such a talent should have a larger audience. He and Mrs. Field nicknamed her "Flo the First" and decided that she was a once-famous singer who had come from Paris and sung to wild applause in the old French Opera House—but life and love and liquor had taken their sorry toll.

They outlined this to the old woman, taught her the names of some of the more familiar operas, a few poses, and a few bits of melody. Thereafter, when Flo took a group through the quarter, sooner or later "Flo the First" showed up. The group had already been prepared for the tragic story, and she would go into her act. If she mixed Camile with Carmen, or Marguerite with Manon, it did not matter. "The mind," Flo or Saxon would say with a pathetic shrug.

Convinced that here at last they had seen the living evidence of what had been a romantic and fascinating past, the tourists gave generously to the old gal, who certainly enjoyed at least one highly successful operatic season.

Between newspaper jobs in New Orleans, Saxon worked briefly in Chicago. At this time there seems to have been danger of his becoming tubercular. He was far too thin, he began running a temperature every afternoon, and, finally, the doctors ordered a rest in a suitable climate. He went to the "ozone belt" in Louisiana, a place of sandy streams, pine trees, and sulphur springs, and boarded in the home of an old lady and her two middle-aged maiden daughters. Although physically he must have been feeling very low, he enjoyed his stay, made some money by editing a special issue of the local newspaper, and afterwards told many stories concerning the household.

The old lady was in her dotage, but she had fitful recollections of past glories. Frequently, from what seemed to be a deep reverie, she would break out with some exciting tale. Also, she had a robust approach to life that was often in conflict with the more genteel attitudes of her daughters.

In order to get the full benefit of the fresh air, Saxon slept on the back porch on an improvised bed made with a mattress and a spring. This was an arrangement which the old lady somehow never succeeded in understanding. Almost daily she would exclaim: "Have we no beds? Have we no bedrooms in this house? Must our guests always be reduced to sleeping on pallets on the floor?"

Sometimes the cats, of which there were many, would get to the back porch early in the morning and curl up along with Saxon. This would also upset the old lady, who predicted that one day alligators from the swamps would be doing the same thing, if he went on with what, she insisted, was merely a foolish whim.

In the late afternoons the four of them would sit on the front porch in rockers—the old lady lost in a dream, Saxon wrapped up against whatever dangers might be about in the "night air," and the "girls" busy reading the society news from New Orleans or embroidering away on a doily. Suddenly the old lady would give her thigh a resounding slap and cry out: "Three husbands have I had, fine bucks all." And while her daughters murmured, "Oh, Mother, dear Mother," she would launch into a none-too-reticent recital of the good times she had had with one or the other of the three.

Another phrase which often emerged from her day-dreams and started her off on tales which she loved to tell over and over was: "I had a tame bear once, but he ran away." The tame bear reminded her of other things, and then there was no telling in what direction she would wander. At other times she would suddenly turn to Saxon and inquire: "Have you ever met my daughter Louise?" She continued to do this after Saxon had been there for weeks and had seen Louise (whom he had known for years) every day and all day long.

Although she had difficulty in walking, the old lady was too proud to use a cane. She got around the house by lunging from one piece of furniture to the other or by using an umbrella or a broom turned upside down. She was also very proud of her former skill as a horsewoman and was always threatening to sneak away and go for a ride. One day her horrified daughters found her on the dusty highway, hobbling along with the aid of a broom and screaming at an old friend, a Confederate veteran who was astride a broken-down mare: "I'll beat you yet when I get a horse, old man. I'll beat you yet!"

On another occasion during Saxon's stay, there was a bad thunderstorm. The daughters were deathly afraid of lightning and thunder and, as the storm grew worse, one took refuge in a clothes closet, the other got into bed and pulled the covers over her head.

But neither thunder, lightning, wind, nor rain held any terror for the old lady. Pleased for once to be free from constant supervision, she went on a trip of exploration. The attic was a place where she had not been for years, and she decided that this would be a good time to see how it looked. It was reached by a ladder that led to a trap door in the ceiling. How she got up there alone no one will ever know; but somehow she managed and spent a delightful afternoon among relics of the past—trying on old costumes, looking through ancient albums, and in general having herself a time.

The storm over, the girls emerged from their hiding places. Saxon, who had been trying to read, came out of his room. But the old lady was not to be found. They cried out for mother. There was no answer. They searched the house, the gardens, and the surrounding countryside; they telephoned the neighbors, and called upon the police—all without result. Then there was much weeping and wailing. The girls were sure that mother had wandered out into the storm and was now lying dead in a gulley. At last, considering the fact that they had searched everywhere else, someone suggested the attic. There they found mother, wearing a hat that had been discarded thirty years before, sitting in a dusty arm-chair that had only one leg, and engrossed in an old bound copy of *The Southern Gentlewoman.*

Although she had managed to get up there by herself, it took the combined efforts of Saxon, the girls, and several neighbors to get her down. After hysterical reunions and after the neighbors had departed, peace settled once more on the household. The four of them were once again sitting, quietly rocking on the porch; Louise, whose lamentations had been the loudest, occasionally wiped back tears as she remembered the ordeal of the afternoon. For almost a half-hour the old lady sat, as if in a trance, probably thinking about the wonderful things she had found in the attic. Then suddenly she turned to Saxon and said: "Have you ever met my daughter Louise?"

When, after a surprisingly short time he seemed quite well again, Saxon returned to New Orleans to become a feature writer for the newspapers, a dashing young man about town, and eventually, through his magazine articles, short stories, and books, the best known interpreter of Louisiana in general, and New Orleans in particular, of his generation. During most of his time in the city he lived in the French Quarter.

The French Quarter in the twenties witnessed, as did Greenwich Village, although, to be sure, on a smaller scale, an interesting renascence in literature and art. Here, at various times, lived a large number of people who later were to become well-known. A magazine called *The Double Dealer* made its appearance as one of the important "little magazines" of the time, and soon artists and writers were crowding into every old house and slave quarter. Among those who were in and out of New Orleans during this time were Sherwood Anderson, William Faulkner, Thomas Wolfe, Oliver LaFarge, Roark Bradford, "Pop" Hart, Arnold Genthe, Hamilton Basso, Frans Blom, John McClure, Richard Kirk, Nathalie Scott, Charles Bien, Caroline Durieux, Genevieve Pitot, Kenneth Knobloch, Alberta Kinsey, and Bill Spratling.

In 1925 Covarrubias did a book of caricatures of New York and Hollywood celebrities called *The Prince of Wales and Other Famous Americans.* Bill Spratling and Bill Faulkner, then comparatively unknown, did a slim book in the same manner called *Sherwood Anderson and Other Famous Creoles* (1926), caricaturing most of the people mentioned above. Saxon was shown reclining with great eclat against an elaborately embroidered cushion reading a copy of *Eminent Victorians*; the caption for his caricature read: "The Mauve Decade in St. Peter Street."

Saxon particularly admired Sherwood Anderson, whom he thought the greatest American writer of his generation, and was pleased to have had on one occasion a chance to help Anderson in an unusual way. Anderson was then living in the Quarter and was expecting a visit from one of his publishers. He believed that if he could impress that gentleman with what seemed to be a state of comparative affluence, it would be possible to get an advance of the size he wanted. He decided a display of old Southern elegance was what was needed and that a fine old four-posted bed would do the trick. Saxon had a fine old four-posted bed. It was duly carted out of his house and down the street and around the corner; and Mr. Anderson got his advance.

On one of Thomas Wolfe's visits in the Quarter, he took his clothes to a small Chinese laundry in the neighborhood, promptly lost his ticket, and forgot the name and location of the laundry. He came to Saxon with his problem. Could he remember the street it was on? asked Saxon. He could not. Could he remember what the building looked like? He could not. Could he remember anything at all that would identify the place? Wolfe thought for sometime and in all seriousness said: "Well, as I recall, Lyle, there was a big black cat sitting out in front of the door."

During this period Saxon restored his first house in the French Quarter. He had always loved this old section of New Orleans, which at that time had fallen on evil days. The Creoles who built its handsome homes had either died off, or become impoverished, or moved uptown to more fashionable neighborhoods. Many of the old houses had been converted into tenements (a calf grew to maturity upstairs in one of the famous Pontalba Buildings), cheap bars, honky-tonks, and brothels; others had been heedlessly torn down to make room for factories, parking lots, and undistinguished modern buildings. There was even, at one time, a movement among a group of citizens to tear down the entire Quarter, as a rat-infested slum not in keeping with their views as to what a city should be.

Saxon was among the first to take up the defense of the Quarter and was one of the leaders in the movement to restore the old buildings. This finally culminated in the entire city's realization that the Quarter is its greatest architectural heritage and, even more than the Mardi Gras, and the famous restaurants, its greatest tourist attraction.

The house was at 536 Royal Street. Saxon did nothing to the original lines of the building, but simply cleaned the place up and removed the unsightly partitions which cut the spacious rooms into rabbit warrens. Then he furnished it with antique pieces of the kind treasured by the Creoles. Perhaps what the people who visited him at this house most vividly recall was the elaborate Victorian parlor furniture, upholstered in red. In a room with white walls and ceilings, black woodwork and floors, and red damask curtains, it was

W. C. Odiorne

COURTYARD OF THE ROYAL STREET HOUSE
— French Quarter, New Orleans

displayed with great effect. One of his other prized pieces was a chandelier that had once hung in the salon of a Mississippi steamer.

Eventually the house became something of a showplace, and through it passed many people. Minnie Maddern Fiske, who was born in New Orleans, was one of the visitors for whom Saxon had a great fondness. Having heard about the house, she wanted to see it and said she would come after an evening performance of *Miss Nelly of N'Orleans,* if Saxon would provide her with an oyster loaf and a bottle of wine. (An oyster loaf consists of half a loaf of French bread, toasted and buttered, filled with Louisiana oysters fried in the New Orleans manner. It is something that no native New Orleanian can resist.)

Mrs. Fiske arrived in the costume of the last act but, as was her custom, completely swathed in veils, and brought along an old Creole woman who had been her French teacher as a child. Together with Noel Straus, who at that time also worked on *The Times-Picayune* and shared the Royal Street house, they sat up half the night talking and reminiscing. Mrs. Fiske said, among other things, that she never again wanted to play tragedy: it took too much out of her—life had been grim enough. This made a lasting impression on Saxon. When, a number of years later, he saw her in a revival of Ibsen's *Ghosts,* he said she almost succeeded in turning *that* into a comedy—dismissing Pastor Manders as if she just wished the old bore would go away and let her get back to a good novel, and replying to Oswald in a manner that implied she thought the sun a rather vulgar thing to have asked for—that a true child of hers would have preferred the moon.

[135]

When they decided to leave, it was raining and quite late. After they were settled in a cab, Mrs. Fiske suggested they take her old teacher home first. But the lateness of the hour and the strength of the wine or the general excitement had bemused the old lady; when they reached her neighborhood, she forgot where she lived. They went up one muddy street and down the next, while the cab driver cursed and the old lady changed her mind; and it grew later and later. Mrs. Fiske had a matinée the next day and everybody was pretty much worn out. Finally, they came to a street which the old lady decided was the right one. It was in such condition that the driver was afraid to chance it and, since she said she lived just off the corner, Saxon himself took her to her door while Mrs. Fiske and Noel remained in the cab. "Well," said Mrs. Fiske when he returned, with a certain amount of asperity, remembering the matinée not many hours off, "and where *did* the sweet old thing live? Or did she just go off on a broom?"

Saxon first met Sister Anastasia while he was still a reporter. She was a Negro nun, then already in her middle years, a large, distinguished-looking woman with a great zest for life and a great compassion for humanity.

One day, when a small tramp-steamer from some European port docked at a wharf not far from Canal Street, New Orleans, it was discovered that some of the crew had already died of the bubonic plague; two others were dangerously ill with the dread disease. And there was not, in all of the city, anyone who would volunteer to nurse the stricken seamen until Sister Anastasia came forward. Saxon, admiring her courage, wrote a newspaper story about her. This was the beginning of a long friendship.

Sister Anastasia is a member of the Convent of the Sisters of the Holy Family, a school for Negro children conducted by Negro nuns. The convent occupies a building on Orleans Street just off Royal. It is an interesting irony of New Orleans life that in the nineteenth century the same building housed the famous quadroon balls.

The Order to which Sister Anastasia belonged is vowed to poverty, and the nuns frequently did small jobs of sewing and darning in order to make money to buy certain necessities and improvements for the convent. Saxon worked out an arrangement for Sister Anastasia to do his mending. At his house on Royal Street, a few blocks from the convent, she would call once a week, always accompanied by a smaller and lighter-complexioned nun, who remained as a quiet background for the good Anastasia's more exuberant personality.

Then a little ceremony would be performed. The clothes to be mended would be ready in a bundle in the living room; on the table would be a decanter with wine or liqueur and three glasses. After the nuns were seated, Saxon would fill the glasses and offer the refreshments to them. They would thank him but explain that one of the rules of their Order was that the nuns could not eat or drink in the company of lay persons. Saxon would then apologize for having forgotten this rule and ask permission to drink his own drink. He would do this while the conversation went on and would move the tray and the other two filled glasses to a side table. Later he would suddenly remember something else that needed mending and, excusing himself, disappear into the bedroom where he could be heard rummaging among the drawers and closets. After a short time he would return with a shirt or a pair of socks and there would be more conversation before the nuns left. No one ever looked in the direction of the tray; but always, at the end of these meetings, there were three empty glasses.

Sister Anastasia once told Saxon that she suffered from weak arches. Since he himself had difficulty in getting shoes that were comfortable, he could sympathize with her and recommended a special kind of arch-preserver shoes. These were expensive, however, and knowing the limited amount of money at the disposal of the nuns, he offered to "keep" Sister Anastasia in shoes. There were, of course, protestations; but eventually Saxon had his way. Once a year, thereafter, she would call him to say she was going to get a pair. Later she would call again to thank him and report on the quality and the fit. Still later, among his incoming bills one would be found marked: "Shoes for Negro nun."

One day I came into Saxon's office and he was laughing into the telephone. Then he said: "Just a minute Sister, would you mind repeating what you just told me?"

When I picked up the receiver, she was still chuckling. After we had exchanged greetings, she said: "I just called Mr. Saxon to thank him and to give him a report on how the new shoes felt. I got them yesterday afternoon and I put them on the first thing this morning. But about three o'clock, while I was sitting in the courtyard watching the little girls play basketball, they began to feel tight and I began to feel a little tired. Nothing wrong, you know. Just new shoes and the fact that I'm not as young as I used to be. So sitting and watching the children, I unlaced them and slipped them off. And my feet felt so good that when they started to pester me to play with them, I got up and did. You know what happened? I made three goals."

The thought of the amiable Anastasia in her stocking feet, her ample body enveloped by a flowing nun's habit, and her kind black face shining as she made three goals, was too much for us all. And suddenly the three of us were laughing.

Nuns always possessed a certain fascination for Saxon. As small boys, he and George Favrot delighted in teasing those at the convent school near their home in Baton Rouge. Once they planned a midnight roll-call for the boarding students. And, as the boys called out from behind a tree across the road—"Bessie Mae Swan, Dora Thea Hettwer, Mary Allerton Fiske, Elizabeth Adele Townson, Micaela Phelan Hickey," girls, screaming "Present!" and "Here!" rushed out in their nightdresses onto the balconies that encircled the building, their pigtails and *papillotes* bobbing up and down in excitement.

On another occasion they dressed up two stone angels who guarded the entrance to the chapel, where the nuns heard mass, as street-walkers—complete with feathered hats, fur neckpieces, pocketbooks, and much too much lip rouge.

There is one other story concerning nuns that might be worth the telling: Some thirty years ago the Ursuline Convent, which for almost two centuries had played a leading part in the education of the young girls of the city, found that its enrollment was beginning to drop off. Parents had begun to think of the convent as not quite up to date. The nuns, determined to keep abreast of the times, announced the establishment of a modern gymnasium, a facility which the institution had previously lacked. Saxon covered the story and spent one entire day visiting the nuns in the convent. It was a day he often recalled with pleasure and as a memento he kept a photograph of himself surrounded by nuns.

The idea of such a gymnasium struck him, however, as having humorous possibilities, and he amused himself by inventing a musical comedy called *The Nuns' Gymnasium.* Part of this he wrote down, but most of it he kept in his head. There were dance routines, group numbers, and solos—all highly entertaining. I can remember one evening at the Bradfords' when, to music improvised by Mary Rose Bradford, we acted out various parts of the comedy under the direction of Saxon, who also played a leading rôle. Roark Bradford, Caroline Durieux, Arthur MacArthur, and several others took part. The hit song of the evening was one that began: "I'm a travelling sister looking 'round for heathen men."

Whether he interviewed Negro nuns or famous actresses, figures of international importance or the Russian immigrant who sold balloons in City Park, Saxon usually managed to have fun.

At the time when he was looking for furnishings for the house on Royal Street (one of the things he wanted but seemed unable to find was a peacock chair made of woven cane), a particularly violent murder took place in downtown New Orleans. Saxon arrived at the scene of the crime to find the police questioning a tough-looking but frightened little man in a shabby room that gave evidence of a violent fracas. The corpse still lay on the floor, and most of the furniture had been broken into bits; in one corner stood a beautiful peacock chair, intact but spattered with blood.

Saxon's first question when he had a chance to talk to the man the police were accusing of murder was: "Where did you get that chair?" He knew that such chairs were sometimes made by prisoners in places like Manila and thought it might possibly lead to a clue; but he admitted that the desire to own such a chair was uppermost in his mind. The chair did figure in the trial, though mostly for local color, and in the end Saxon purchased it from the little man who had by then become a friend. Cleaned and scrubbed, it stood in the enclosed patio of the Royal Street house.

Occasionally, a visitor sitting there, admiring the house and its furnishings, would say: "And this chair, Mr. Saxon, where did it come from?" Saxon liked to reply: "The first time I saw that chair it was covered with the blood of a man who got hacked into pieces by a friend who found him cheating with his wife."

Saxon used to tell this story about Gwen Bristow, the novelist, then a cub reporter: Gwen was covering her first murder, a gruesome affair in which the head, arms, and legs of a woman had been cut from the body and stuffed into a trunk. When she got to the scene, they were just being removed. But she was determined to be brave and hold her own. So in a hardboiled manner that was only surface, she burst into a popular song of the day—"I Ain't Got No Body." Then she went out into the courtyard and was quietly sick.

[141]

Occasionally Saxon's newspaper assignments proved dangerous. This was particularly true when, during a campaign to oust a long-intrenched and corrupt city government, *The Times-Picayune* ran a series of articles called *A Thousand and One Nights in New Orleans*. These were exposés of gangster rackets running the usual gamut from gambling to white slavery and traffic in narcotics. There was even one article on a girls' school in the city where the pupils were "on call" for a bordello around the corner.

Although the articles were unsigned, Saxon wrote many of them. Some of the racketeers recognized him and there were several attempts on his life. His friends, worried, began bringing pistols and shotguns to the Royal Street house and presently he possessed a small arsenal. Finally his enemies, having exhausted fake traffic accidents and the like, even tried voodoo. One morning he woke to find a crude doll riddled with pins and needles in his pillow. Against the warning of Noel Straus, he couldn't resist showing it to the Negro maid, Alice Grinner. And Alice promptly left town to visit "sick kinfolk" in Baton Rouge. It was weeks before they were well enough to permit her return.

III

Sometime later Saxon met Mrs. Cammie Garrett Henry (to whom he dedicated *Old Lousiana*) and restored an eighteenth century cabin, once a slave hospital, on her plantation at Melrose, near Natchitoches, Louisiana. This he used for many years as a place to write and as a refuge;

some of his happiest days were spent here. Aunt Cammie, not a blood relation, was one of his most devoted friends.

Although the cabin was a simple building, the interior, under the Saxon influence, acquired a certain elegance, with white panelling, antique furniture, books, and pictures. At the back was a semi-circular garden fenced off from the cotton fields by a screen of banana trees. Saxon planned it as a white garden, which would be at its best at night, and on which he could look out, beyond the large expanse of lawn, to white lilies, moon flowers, and altheas bright under the Melrose moon. On another side of the cabin was a large mint bed planted with a variety of mints for juleps. The bed, appropriately enough, was outlined with alternate whiskey and milk-of-magnesia bottles.

Near this bed, Saxon rigged up an impromptu shower when the bathroom in the cabin was still under construction. One summer morning, while he was scrubbing away, he heard feminine giggles coming from behind the screen of shrubbery. Recognizing the voice of one of the plantation Negroes he called out: "What are you doing prying around here, Mattie? You've had three husbands and eleven children, there's certainly nothing around here you haven't seen before." Overcome with laughter and running away with her apron thrown over her face, Mattie called back: "Yassuh, Mr. Lyle. But I ain't never seen it white."

Aunt Cammie conducted her own gardening on a grand scale—moving full-grown trees from one place to another, or putting in two thousand irises at a time. She was a woman with a tremendous amount of energy and intellectual curiosity, who not only raised a large family, managed a plantation, and planted an incredible garden, but also collected one of the best private libraries on Louisiana, compiled a valuable series of scrapbooks of Louisiana items, bought looms and learned to weave from old patterns, and collected slave cabins and other early structures from the surrounding countryside to be preserved on her own property as guest houses.

An endlessly busy woman, she sometimes wrote letters with one hand while watering flowers with the other. The letters were telegraphic, usually containing certain stock phrases and clichés which she had picked up over the years. One of these was: "This too will pass," which she always used after relating one of the more violent upheavals on the plantation. Another that Saxon was fond of quoting was first used in commenting on a difficulty that had arisen between two of their friends: "An old trouble," she wrote, "which I thought long since healed, has proved but a smouldering volcano."

Her letters were always warm invitations, urging him to come to Melrose. "Hurry home," she would say, "doors always open. You need rest." Frequently such messages were written on the outside of the envelopes of letters addressed to him at Melrose which she forwarded to New Orleans.

Saxon delighted to tease her and would sometimes reply, imitating her style, or write letters to a few friends who knew them both, signing her name. This, for instance, he scribbled on the back of a letter addressed to a friend in his care which he forwarded:

> Come home. Roof always open. Can't hardly wait. Chickens and children dying. I don't care. This too will pass. Love.
> *Aunt Cammie*

Saxon liked to show off Melrose to his friends and he and Aunt Cammie both enjoyed what they called their "Cane River Tour." Cane River passes in front of Melrose, but the opposite bank is lined with farms of mulattoes who have held this property for almost two centuries. Originally descendants of early French and Spanish settlers, they were always free people of color. Some of them in the eighteenth century owned large plantations and a considerable number of Negro slaves.

Perhaps the best known of the mulatto planters was Grandpère Augustin, an ancestor of Mme. Aubert Rocque. Mme. Aubert Rocque owned a life-sized portrait of Grandpère, painted by one Feuille, a traveling artist who had executed the likeness in 1835; but it was badly torn and in need of restoration. She made an agreement with Saxon, in exchange for certain things she wanted, to give him the portrait to be kept as a piece of Americana. It was carefully restored and hung in his cabin at Melrose. Grandpère Augustin, a fine figure of a mulatto gentleman of the time, stood on a floor of black and white marble against a background of red draperies, pointing with pride to the church he had given to the mulatto community.

Saxon's cabin contained a number of such Negro and mulatto portraits. Perhaps the most interesting of these was one painted by Jules Lion (who flourished in Louisiana between 1830 and 1845), which showed a white planter with his arm proudly and affectionately around the shoulder of a young man said to be his mulatto son.

Saxon wrote a prize winning story called *Cane River* and later a novel about the mulatto community, *Children of Strangers* (1937).

IV

Between 1926 and 1932, Saxon kept an apartment on Christopher Street in New York and spent from five to six months a year there, usually arriving in the late summer and leaving before or shortly after Christmas for Melrose or New Orleans.

This was the period of his greatest literary activity. He had short stories in the *O'Henry Memorial Collection* (1926) and the *O'Brien Collection* (1927) and four books appeared in rapid succession: *Father Mississippi* (1927), *Fabulous New Orleans* (1928), *Old Louisiana* (1929), and *Lafitte, the Pirate* (1930).

He came to know, naturally, a great many people in New York's literary circles: the Benèts and Elinor Wylie, Edmund Wilson and John Dos Passos, Henry Seidel Canby and Ford Maddox Ford. Yet he also knew, as always, an incredibly wide variety of people who had nothing to do with literary life, and his apartment was usually filled with a heterogeneous collection of people, out of which he somehow managed to achieve entertaining and agreeable evenings.

Soon after the success of *Fabulous New Orleans*, he found himself at a party sitting between two charming women. One was the late Alma (Mrs. Paul) Ellerby, and the other Fleta Campbell Springer (Mrs. Robert Coe). But they had not actually been introduced and Saxon had no idea who they were. They knew who he was, however, and as a young author up from the deep South they decided to give him a going over.

They asked him what writers of the moment he particularly liked. He replied that, among others, there was Fleta Campbell Springer, by whose stories in *Harper's* he had been greatly impressed. "Never heard of her," said Alma. "I'll bet she can't write at all," said Fleta. Saxon thereupon went into a great defense of the works of Miss Springer, citing story after story and detail after detail to prove his points and urging both of the ladies to read her. Finally Alma said: "Well, Fleta, my girl, I guess this *is* your day," and explained who they were.

Saxon was overcome with embarrassment, and Fleta said: "Look, Mister; either you are the smoothest number I ever saw come up from that dear old Dixieland or maybe you really like my stuff. Those were mighty sweet words, suh. You come have a drink with me some night soon and we'll talk ourselves out. If we still like each other after that, fine. If not, we'll have saved six months." So he did and they were great friends for the rest of his life. It was Fleta who later said, when some young lady was suffering in his direction from unrequited love and making something of a display of it: "Of course, Lyle always has some woman or other swooning away in his background."

Saxon also admired Elinor Wylie and liked to recall the manner in which she handled a catty woman at a literary tea. Miss Wylie, who was lovely to look at, was also quite nearsighted; but she refused to wear glasses on such an occasion. The woman in question approached her and said: "Is it true, dear Miss Wylie, that you suffer from nearsightedness?" "Yes," said Miss Wylie, "from where I am standing there are many people in the room I can hardly make out. As a matter of fact, my dear, as near as I am to you (peering down closely at the other woman) I can't see *you* at all!"

Other good friends of this period included Doris Ullman, the photographer, Harold Berman, Josiah Titzell, Bill and Dorothy Johnston, Earl Chapman May and Stella Burke May, Rachel Field, and Julia Peterkin. It was Rachel Field who introduced him to the New England countryside, and he was surprised how often it reminded him of the South. This was particularly true when the vogue for Greek Revival architecture, so widespread in the early nineteenth century, suddenly presented to his pleased eyes a house in a New England setting that seemed almost identical with something he knew in Louisiana or Mississippi. He got along well with the New Englanders he met and seemed to think that in many ways they had much in common with the people of the deep South. The difference, he enjoyed saying, was that in New England people in the end just dried up, whereas in the South they simply fell apart.

There were two evenings with Mrs. Peterkin he often remembered. The first was the unfortunate opening night of the play made from her Pulitzer prize-winning novel, *Scarlet Sister Mary*. Miss Ethel Barrymore, in what must certainly have been one of the more notable instances of miscasting in the history of the New York stage, played Sister Mary. Saxon and Mrs. Peterkin endured the performance almost to the bitter end, Mrs. Peterkin retaining her composure, but, he felt, weeping silently within. In the meantime Miss Barrymore, who began the play in blackface, became progressively lighter as one scene followed another; so that by the final curtain she was a pale octoroon. Also, as the play went on, the celebrated Barrymore voice, accustomed to lines considerably different from those that might be spoken by a Gullah Negro, dropped more and more out of character.

Joel Harris (Mrs. Lawrence), who was also present, later used to do an imitation of Miss Barrymore which no one would have enjoyed more than Miss Barrymore herself. Mimicking the famous voice and a number of the more easily recognized mannerisms, Joel would invent high-flown lines that might have been part of a dramatic moment in any one of Miss Barrymore's other highly successful vehicles, ending in a still more highly-flown manner: "And life is life and love is love and there isn't a thing you can do about it"—then lapsing into minstrel-show dialect—"if ya'll axes me."

The other evening he liked to recall was an encounter with Texas Guinan, an old friend of Mrs. Peterkin. The two women were certainly dissimilar in their backgrounds and in the kind of life they led, but each recognized in the other qualities that produced a mutual understanding and respect.

Mrs. Peterkin took Saxon to meet Miss Guinan at a time when her club was at its height and "Hello, suckers" was on everybody's lips. As special friends of Texas Guinan's, they were ushered to a very conspicuous seat and Texas couldn't resist a chance to have fun with the somewhat abashed young gentleman from the South. Suddenly Saxon found himself confronted by a statuesque and seductive blonde wrapped in a long fur cape; but almost as suddenly, while flood lights played on the two of them and all eyes were turned in their direction, the blonde flung aside the cape, revealing a beautiful body ornamented at the moment with only three strategically placed stars. There were cat-calls and whistles and the blowing of horns. For once Saxon seemed at a loss for words.

The New York period was also the period in which Saxon suffered his broken heart. While there was much truth and sincerity in the emotional upset he went through, there was also, he said, some romantic exaggeration. This was, after all, the period of the Lost Generation. Miss Helen Morgan sat on the top of her piano weeping her pretty eyes out over her "Bill" and in the speakeasies all over town anybody who was anybody wept over some "careless love." Saxon was no exception and cried into his Bourbon with the best of them.

Yet, for quite some time, he was seriously affected. He was young and good-looking and popular; he possessed an extraordinary personal charm; his books were praised by the critics; he was making money. But suddenly, he said, none of this was worth anything, and he spent at least one of those New York years in a heavy haze of tears and alcohol.

During this time Fanny Heaslip Lea (an old friend from New Orleans) and Margaret Widdemer, having both just returned from Europe, invited Saxon and a literary gentleman from Texas for dinner. Saxon brought some absinthe, long one of his favorite drinks, and mixed absinthe frappé. Both ladies, after sipping politely, did not find the drink much to their taste, and Saxon and the other man finished off the bottle between them. When, said Saxon, he found himself declaring that both Miss Lea and Miss Widdemer were prostituting their talents writing popular romances and coining money while he, a more serious writer, was

W. C. Odiorne

BEDROOM, ROYAL STREET HOUSE

poverty stricken, he hurriedly said good night and went out to get the train he was taking for the South.

"It seemed," Miss Widdemer later said, "that on the way between New York and New Orleans he got off at every train stop and visited friends. The next day I would receive in the mail a letter from each hostess, the general gist of which was—'Dear Miss Widdemer: Lyle is dreadfully upset. He says he was rude to you and to Miss Lea and is afraid you will never forgive him. Won't you please?' "My own feeling," continued Miss Widdemer, "was that there was nothing I would have liked to have done better, especially in person, but unfortunately I never saw him again.

Later the cause of his broken heart married someone else and much later died. Saxon wrote: "And why, after all these years, should that make me miserable beyond belief?"

V

In October, 1935 Saxon became the State Director for Louisiana of the newly organized Federal Writers' Project, at which time he first met Joe Gilmore. Later he became Regional Consultant for a number of the southern states until, with the help of his good friend Robert Tallant, he closed the projects in 1942. The Louisiana Project produced, along with many items of less general interest, *The New Orleans City Guide,* 1938, *The Louisiana Guide,* 1941, and *Gumbo Ya Ya: A Collection of Louisiana Folk Tales,* 1945.

One fine day in 1938, Saxon had to be rushed off to a hospital for an emergency appendectomy. Being Saxon, this turned out a much more serious operation than it usually is. That appendix made medical history. It was larger than any appendix previously uncovered in all of south Louisiana and it got into places in his anatomy where no Louisiana appendix had ever ventured before. Complications ensued, and for a while his friends had good cause to be alarmed.

But Saxon had an unusual ability to turn trying experiences into amusing ones. Many people can find in retrospect things that are laughable in the difficult times they have encountered. He was one of the few who saw the humorous in tragic or sad things while they were actually happening, who could turn any disaster short of death, and perhaps death itself, into a kind of comedy. In one way or another he managed to get a remarkable amount of fun out of this period of hospitalization. His friends who saw him through it frequently found they were enjoying themselves in spite of their anxiety.

Worried about finances—he had just bought a house—he said in a high fever to one of the trained nurses about something that was to be done for him: "Spare no expense. I care nothing about the expense." And then added as an afterthought: "Not any more than I care about my right eye!"

Later, while he was delirious, the doctors called in a psychiatrist to see if they could go on giving the various drugs that seemed necessary, or if these were having too serious an effect. Saxon's mind, he afterwards said, was a jumble of things real and imagined. At last, however, he realized that what the psychiatrist wanted him to do was to utter a simple declarative sentence, intelligible to the people present. He looked that gentleman straight in the eye and said:

"Once a sonofabitch, always a sonofabitch," and went to sleep.

His condition grew worse. His Catholic friends were having masses said in St. Louis Cathedral and one sneaked a relic of a saint into his room. A Jewish friend's mother was having her favorite rabbi do whatever was orthodox on such an occasion. A Christian-Science practitioner was giving him absent treatment. Probably someplace back-of-town a Negro voodoo doctor was mixing "Johnny the Conquerer Root" with "Long-Life Powder" for an especially potent *gris-gris*.

Early one morning there was a sudden call for a direct blood transfusion. Arthur MacArthur and I were there, but we didn't type; so we got on the telephone and routed friends out of their beds. They all came trooping in to give their blood to Saxon; but one after another they too were rejected. After about ten rejections, Weeks Hall finally proved to be the type needed.

Weeks, one of the best painters in Louisiana, had recently been in an automobile accident in which his painting arm was badly splintered; it was still weak and sore and he had to wear a leather brace. When the cot was arranged next to Saxon's bed for the transfusion, it was the broken arm that was closest to Saxon and into which the intern tried to get the needle.

Saxon, who might easily have been dying, was mumbling incoherently through a fog of fever and dope; the intern was nervous and perspiring; the needles were blunt, and he had to send back three times for new ones—puncturing poor Weeks' sore arm again and again. At last, however, the transfusion began to work. Saxon, who for almost twenty-four hours had been either in a stupor or out of his head, suddenly came to. Recognizing Weeks and taking the situation in at a glance, he said: "If you think this is going to make me *paint* any better, you're crazy."

From that time on Weeks and Lyle, who had been friends for years, called each other cousin. Occasionally they corresponded, pretending they were slave-holding planters of the middle nineteenth century. Here are three of their letters. The volume referred to is the *Louisiana State Guide:*

> 'The Shadows'
> New Iberia, La.

Dear Coz:

Our plantations go moderately well and the yaws among our new Negroes is slackening. It seems, in some way, to be connected with the miasmas of spring.

I hear much from travellers going west, though the roads have been excessively bad, of the new volume which our government in Washington has prepared. I am desirous of purchasing a first copy, though I am not averse to accepting one, especially if it bears your own esteemed dedication.

If it should come on the next packet, I should be obliged. If you occasionally meet Major Dreyer in the Coffee Room, I want to be remembered to him with my respects. I am, Sir

> Obediently yrs,

April 11,   Weeks Hall
(1941)

To the honorable W. W. Hall
The Shadows, New Iberia, Louisiana

Esteemed Cousin:

The post chaise brought your welcome missive on yester eve. I cannot tell you the pleasure it gave me to hear that the plantations go well and that your health improves. But I regret that the blacks are suffering again from the yaws; I consider it a mortification, dear Cousin, from God our Master, but I trust the slaves will become better as the season advances. As for the miasmas rising from the Teche, I cannot bring myself to think that the effluvia does aught save stir indiscreet thoughts, and, alas, perhaps indiscreet actions as well. I remember in my own case, on certain summer evenings . . . but why speak of our gaudy youth, dear Coz, as we approach Life's Sunset?

The news from the Capital is alarming, and I fear that the damned Yankees are planning further trouble. My son has been called to the service of his country. I was glad to offer him, inasmuch as I am now too old to carry a musket as I did in the Mexican War.

I hasten to give you news of your sons. Young Ned Weeks was set aside, due to the family affliction of gout which he has acquired so early in life, but to my surprise, dark Sambo was speedily chosen. What is the country coming to, may I ask? Was not his mother the likely wench which you sold subsequently to General Beauregard?

The publication from Washington, which has been delayed, due to inclement weather, goes forward to you today by pony express as I find that method of communication preferable to the packet in these troubled times. You will find your copy suitably inscribed by Major Dreyer (who asks, too, to be fondly remembered to you), by Captain Wixon, and by

Yr. Obedient Servant and Cousin
Lyle Saxon

Port Hudson, April 15, 1861

'The Shadows'
New Iberia, La.

Dear Coz:

My salutations and my profound acknowledgments of your favor in forwarding to me the volume on our glorious State. That it has not been wrecked by the heirs of our late Senator is due to the grace of God and the efforts of others who are, at last reports, employing newer methods.

One of my breeding Negroes is failing in his powers; indeed, I fear that extramural activities have had much to do with it. His results are as unstable as the propagation, for color, of the Zinnia from seed. The last infant had red hair and was freckled, with much the general conformation of our overseer.

We, up here, feel the war clouds, much as we did before the thunderclap of Sumter, which reminds me that infection from excessive promiscuity might also be termed the Lost Cause.

Old Thomas will await you on your next journey up the Teche with your favorite tall and cold Roffignac. In the meantime, I have the honor to be, in all gratitude,

Your ob'dt servant

W. H.

Wednesday

As a writer of humorous verse as well as humorous and witty letters, Saxon had a considerable reputation among his friends, although many of the verses were either too private, or too Rabelaisian, or both, to be suitable for general circulation. A number of his friends also wrote verses and there were frequent exchanges. Roark Bradford, for instance, used to write a poem for Saxon every Christmas. Like many of Saxon's own compositions, however, they would hardly get by the censors. Rachel Field wrote and illustrated a whole series of charming little books for Saxon containing epitaphs for their mutual acquaintances and other poems.

During the lifetime of the Writers' Project, whenever Saxon or I felt the danger of losing our tempers, we would take five minutes out to write a limerick. Frequently we made it into a contest. The results sometimes seemed to us to bear the unmistakable marks of genius, but almost always they were for a private audience.

Saxon's early training as a reporter had made him an avid reader of newspapers, always on the lookout for unusual items. These he would frequently clip and mail to his friends, along with verses and drawings inspired by the clippings. For example:

> Marjorie Hindsmarch, aged four, of Preston, England, was killed when a stone cross fell from the top of a gravestone in North Shields Cemetery where she had gone to place flowers on her father's grave.

NOT POLLYANNA

> *Now Marjorie was young and fat—*
> *The cross fell down and squashed her flat*
> *Yes, squashed her skin and bone!*
> *She broke the only neck she had,*
> *It served her right, for she was bad,*
> *She should have frolicked with the glad*
> *And let the cross alone!*

He was quick to grasp the mannerisms of popular poets and parody them. At a time when Edna St. Vincent Millay's *A Few Figs from Thistles* was much in the news, he wrote to a sick friend:

Dear ——:

> I'm just in town for the day, and wanted to look you up, but hearing that you were ill, I am writing this note instead. I wrote this poem especially for you—I think it is the best thing I have ever done. . . . don't you? It contains all my best ideas —or rather, let us say—all my favorite themes.

[157]

So sorry to have missed seeing you while in New Orleans.
Much love from

E. St. V. M-ll-y

ALACK-A-DAY

I trimmed a hat for kitty, but the damned cat wouldn't wear it—
She said it wasn't stylish and she scampered down the lane,
Where she met my sailor lover, and he recognized the bonnet,
So he put her on a schooner and he's carried her to Spain.

The neighbors sit and gossip and they say: "She's lost her kitty,
Her lovely little pussy with an intellect immense."
I sit and sleep and bake and sweep, but ah it is a pity
That kitty took my bonnet—for it cost ten cents.

He's gone, my sailor lover, and its little that he's caring,
He's sailing off with Kitty (for he thinks that Kitty's me!)
And it's little that I'm caring for the dress that I am wearing,
For I'm committing suicide at half-past three!

This was his description of a pretentious female of his
acquaintance:

> *She has the bear's ethereal grace,*
> *The bland hyena's laugh,*
> *The footsteps of an elephant,*
> *The neck of a giraffe*
>
> *She's really very charming*
> *(Though my heart its passion hides),*
> *She's all my fancy painted her,*
> *But Christ! how much besides!*

On an invitation to the wedding of an acquaintance who
was marrying a man named Oldfather, he quickly scribbled:

John L. Herrmann
GRANDPA'S BED, SAXON'S ROOM – *St. Charles Hotel, New Orleans*

"You are Oldfather William," the young bride said,
"And your hair has become very white,
And yet you incessantly get in my bed,
Do you think, at your age, it is right?"

On a sentimental South-American postcard, picturing two foolish-looking angels flying over a towered city, he wrote:

I seen two angels fly over the city
What a pity! What a pity!
I thought at first that they was negotiable
But they flown too high to be very sociable.

A New Orleans man he knew committed suicide by jumping out of a hotel window into a busy street. Distressed, we were talking about the unhappy incident with an elderly woman friend. "I do wish, if he *had* to do it, he had not jumped where he could have hurt someone," Saxon said. "He might at least have jumped in an alley." "Well, *I* would never jump in an alley," said our friend, meaning, I suppose, that she would not commit suicide at all, but sounding as though she were too socially prominent for alleyways. Saxon immediately began to tease her about this and we all felt better. Sometime later he wrote the following:

GLOOMY TUESDAY

Not that window, Saxon
(Try to keep this neat)
This one's to the alley,
That to Royal Street.

The cops said that his bones all cracked
(Do this thing with dash!)

[159]

Other people's bones may crack,
I shall only splash.

I hear voices singing,
It's the angel's choir,
Or perhaps the taunting
Voice of Eddie Dreyer.

How shall I dress up for this?
Slack suit or pajama?
I'll be funny either way. . . .
God, I want my mama.

The following was written while Saxon was on a trip to Arkansas to straighten out details concerning the *Arkansas Guide:*

Although I have not traveled far
I do not care for Arkansas
Nor for my state of health.
My multiplicity of woe
Is caused by soreness of my toe
And by my lack of wealth.

Today I limp along the ways,
Sighing for healthy, gaudy days
That I enjoyed in youth:
My flashing smile, my dancing feet
My narrow thighs, oh joy complete!
Where are they now, forsooth?

Now, as my eyes grow dim and shifty
And I approach the age of fifty
This thought cuts like a knife:
It makes me mad, it makes me furious
To find that I'm no longer curious
About the facts of life.

So gather your rosebuds while ye may,
That's what I always, always say.

As a preface for Olive Leonhardt's devastating book of drawings on New Orleans, called *New Orleans, Drawn and Quartered,* he wrote:

The pen of Olive Leonhardt
Has a cruel catlike touch
It drips with gall and venom
Lewdness, lechery, and such.
The result is simply awful
And I like it very much.

The poem which he quoted most was written, he said, at the ripe age of twenty:

Life is a difficult thing at best,
Conditions here should be deplored,
Life is God's most subtle jest,
And I'm bored, bored, bored.

On the occasion of his fiftieth birthday he added a second stanza:

For thirty long years I've felt this way,
Wormwood and gall to boot,
Wine, women, and song
Didn't last me long
And now I taste bitter fruit.

It was for this birthday that the Bradfords decided to give a party and their mulatto cooks, Louise and Lucille, outdid themselves in the preparation of food. On the evening of the party the guests sat around eating and drinking in the Bradford courtyard on Toulouse Street in the French Quarter. Everyone had done his best to produce something amusing for Saxon. Burdette Huggins and Barbara Brooks (Mrs. Nancy Barton Guion) arrived carrying a huge spray of flowers with a card from one of New Orleans' tackiest funeral parlors. It trailed long purple streamers on which was written in gold: "Eventually, Why not now?" Bill Glasscock came with a potted century plant which had been cut down the center. He explained that it was "a half-a-century plant." Hazel Breaux made an appearance dressed to represent Saxon's favorite heroine "Ada" in his story, *The Centaur Plays Croquet.* Complete with a croquet mallet and a bustle, she baffled one or two of the more literal-minded guests. Tess and Bob Crager, whom Saxon liked to tease about the esoteric items in their private library, threatened to print a "very private" edition of *The Life and Times of Lyle Saxon.*

But Mrs. Leo Spofford was responsible for the best joke of the evening.

Saxon, who at the time weighed well over two hundred pounds, used to tell a story which had been told to him by his grandfather. It concerned an old Southern Colonel who, by eating too much gumbo and drinking too many mint juleps, got fatter and fatter, until he could no longer tie his shoelaces. Eventually there were a number of other things he could no longer do; so he had two little Negro boys in attendance and, on the occasion when he needed certain kinds of assistance, he would clap his hands and they would come running. The story had a bawdy ending. Saxon told it extremely well.

By the time it was almost midnight, everyone was exhausted with laughing at the foolishness that had been going on. We thought that there would be no more tricks that night. Then Leo skillfully maneuvered so that she and Saxon were sitting on a small bench in the center of the rear end of the courtyard and, as the St. Louis Cathedral clock chimed the last stroke of twelve, she clapped her hands. Out of nowhere rushed two little black boys, clad in nothing except white loin cloths, one carrying a quart of Bourbon, the other the kind of bedroom receptacle the little boys had carried in Grandpa's story. They presented both to Saxon with elaborate ceremony while the cooks, whose nephews they were and who had kept them quiet and amused upstairs all evening, doubled up with laughter in the doorway.

The ability of Saxon to laugh at himself was always evident. At a civic function in New Orleans, after one of the speakers in his praise of native writers had been carried away with local pride and Creole exuberance, Meigs Frost turned to Saxon and said: "Well, as I always say, Lyle, so many of us here are internationally famous locally." This became a phrase Saxon often repeated when visitors gushed (as they frequently did) over his works.

At a literary party given in his honor in New Orleans, a fluttering woman congratulated him and told how much she had enjoyed his latest book; but, lest he take her for someone too easily won, or not given to serious consideration of such matters, added that she really preferred his preceding book. "Yes," she repeated, to emphasize her critical acumen, "*Old Man Adam and His Chillun* is really your best book to date." Roark Bradford, the author of *Old Man Adam and His Chillun*, was within earshot and heard Saxon, who winked at him over the dear lady's plumes, say that she was perfectly right and he too agreed that *Old Man Adam* was the best thing he had done.

Fabulous New Orleans and *Old Louisiana* went on selling year after year, and there was always a great demand for Saxon's autograph from visitors who were discovering the City and the State for the first time through his eyes. He was gracious about the autographing, but joked about it. "I started out to be a writer," he would say, "and ended up as a souvenir."

Because he was quite fair game, his friends occasionally teased him on this subject. Once an imaginary edition of *Fabulous New Orleans* was planned: it was to have a praline in a pocket on the inside of the back cover. Another story had it that an unsigned copy of this book reposed under a bell glass in the *Cabildo*, the old Spanish government building in New Orleans, now a historical museum. It was the only known *unautographed* copy. On still another occasion an itinerant printer set up shop near the St. Charles Hotel and printed a newspaper in which one could have any given headline added in type four inches high. Saxon amused himself by having inserted, in the morning papers of various friends, sheets announcing such interesting news items as: *Alberta Kinsey Finds Baby on Doorstep, Joyce Michell Joins Marines, Alma Hammond Tells All.* But no one was more pleased than he to receive an "Extra" early one morning proclaiming: *Saxon Stuffed for Cabildo.*

There was also an imaginary organization called the "Lyle Club." Its membership was made up, without their knowing it, of people who met him for the first time and would say: "Dear Mr. Saxon, I have heard so much about you, I have often looked forward to this" and, two minutes later, were "Lyle-ing" him all over the place, as if they had known him from infancy.

The fad of using the first initial and the full middle name (often a family name) annoyed Saxon. In the early days of the Writers' Project there was a worker named T. Lyall ——— who, somehow or other, irritated Saxon's red-headed secretary Katie. One day when Saxon was teasing her, she flounced out of the room saying: "All right, if that's the way you feel about it, Mr. T. Lyle Saxon." This pleased a number of people, all of whom adopted Katie's invention.

Not long after we were having a drink in the St. Charles Bar, which was then not all chromium and glass as it is now, but a nostalgic place out of the nineties, with mahogany booths, red velvet curtains, and oversized paintings of fleshy, wasp-waisted ladies cavorting about in provocative attitudes. It had been a trying day. The comfort and peace of the bar and a Planters Punch were very welcome.

Presently a woman Saxon had known and liked for a long time came in with another woman, fresh from the battle then raging in Natchez, Mississippi, between the *home-owners'* pilgrimage club and the *garden-owners* club. (We had often pondered the predicament of some poor gal possessed of both a home *and* a garden.) The stranger was the type best described as a "gabby Southern belle." After introductions they both joined us for a drink. Then, as if she had had her lines written for her, our new acquaintance played the part of the perfect candidate for the "Lyle Club." At one moment, she was saying: "Dear Mr. Saxon, I have so looked forward to meeting you," and in almost the same breath: "Lyle, did you ever . . . ?"

After they were gone, we were laughing. We had not noticed, however, that smirking at a nearby table sat Katie of the red hair and a friend of ours named Bill Glasscock, who had a Southern accent to end all Southern accents and whose ancestors had raised enough cane in old Louisiana to get into two of Saxon's books. Suddenly Bill leaned over and in his best drawl said: Dear Mr. T. Lyle Saxon, would you mind very much, suh, if ah just called you plain T?"

From then on, for a number of people, Saxon became plain "T". No one ever knew what "T" stood for and, as a matter of fact, it never stood for anything, though there were the usual ribald suggestions.

VI

The second house in the French Quarter that Saxon restored is at 536 Madison Street, a street just one block long running from Chartres to Decatur. The street was not one of the original ones in the Quarter, but had been cut through at a later date and named in honor of President Madison.

The house, which is the one referred to in *The Friends of Joe Gilmore*, is an interesting combination of Spanish and Creole styles. It runs around three sides of a court, the fourth side of which is backed by the rear wall of the lower Pontalba buildings, erected by Micaela, Baroness Pontalba, in 1849. One wing, built in the eighteenth century, has a series of arches enclosing a loggia, and a wide gallery with a second tier of arches above looking into the courtyard. It was originally part of the old Spanish Barracks. The front of the building had been added sometime later in the nineteenth century. The other wing had been a stable, with slave quarters on the second floor and a balcony also looking down into the courtyard. The part of the building facing the street had a balcony on the second floor with a simple wrought-iron railing, to which later owners have added more elaborate iron work to support a balcony roof.

The house had gone through many stages. The Spanish Barracks part had been, among other things, a barroom and an oyster bar. When Saxon got the place, it was a cheap rooming house with the large old rooms badly cut up, the courtyard cemented over, and rickety wooden runways extending from the upstairs gallery of one wing across the courtyard to the other.

The usual jokes were made about the house and he was even presented with a sign, done in the manner of early tavern signs, lettered with the name: *Saxon's Folly.* There were many other suggestions for names, but the place was usually called the "Pink House," because the stucco and brick of its exterior construction ended up by being painted pink.

Flower beds were laid down in the courtyard, which was green all the year round with bamboo and climbing fig and fragrant with wisteria and sweet olive. It was a very pleasant house, though Saxon never actually managed to live in it as he had planned. He did spend a good deal of time in one apartment or another and the house was the scene of much festivity enjoyed by his friends. The John Steinbecks were married there.

Many of the additions Saxon made to the original house had interesting associations. A carved cypress doorway, which opened at the end of the loggia to a smaller court-yard in the rear, had once been part of an old confessional in the St. Louis Cathedral, removed when the cathedral was restored some years ago. Some of the other doors had been part of an old New Orleans theatre.

Some time after Saxon had acquired the pink house, the house adjoining it was also restored. It was taller than his by a whole story and would have looked down into the courtyard, had it not been that the Creoles, who designed these houses, built "party walls" which provided both privacy and protection against fires. On two occasions in the early history of New Orleans fire destroyed almost the whole of the city, and there was a city ordinance still in effect making it illegal to cut through such walls. Saxon was outraged, and rightly so, therefore, when one day he came down to Madison Street to find a number of windows cut through.

Several years later, during the war, I was in town on a furlough and spent the week-end at the Madison Street house in the apartment that Marge Hunter had been kind enough to let me use in her absence. Saxon had people in for dinner and drinks and conversation, but I had been working rather hard and needed sleep. So at midnight I excused myself and went to bed in the rear bedroom. Two hours later Saxon was shaking me, telling me to get up, that the house next door was on fire and that flames and sparks and smoke were pouring into the courtyard. Half asleep, I agreed and, as he rushed out to attend to something else, turned over and went back to sleep.

About fifteen minutes later he came in and really awak-ened me. When I got out to the court, the scene was frightening and I hurried upstairs to Alice (Mrs. Robert) Willoughby's apartment to see if there were anything I could do to help get things out of the house. Alice, completely self-possessed, was primarily concerned with the safety of her dog Shaddie. Saxon had been very fond of the house and had put practically his last penny into it, but he too was philosophic. "There has been something wrong with this place ever since that woman cut those Goddamned windows," he said. "Let's forget about it and have a drink." So the three of us sat on the balcony overlooking Madison Street with highballs in our hands and Shaddie quiet at his mistress's feet. Smoke and flames continued to pour now out of one opening in the burning house, now out of another; showers of sparks settled on the roof above us from time to time, and we wondered each time if the pink house would soon be ablaze. The firemen were wondering too.

A crowd soon collected in the street below. Among them was Enrique Alferez, the Mexican sculptor, who called up to us. Saxon invited him for a drink saying: "We might as well get some fun out of this, if possible." A few minutes later a man and a woman, who lived in an apartment in the burning building on a level with Mrs. Willoughby's, appeared on their balcony with bundles of clothes and other possessions. We helped the "refugees" transfer their belongings to the Willoughby side and asked them to have a drink. Eventually the balcony was filled with people having a drink, while the house next door continued to burn. Then we remembered that the Guernsey lilies were blooming in the courtyard for the first time and it seemed a shame to have them ruined. Presently the women on the balcony were all wearing Guernsey lillies in their hair. We sat until dawn and at last, when the fire seemed definitely under control and there was no more danger, wandered over to the French Market for coffee and doughnuts.

Somehow the pink house became an unhappy house. Disaster of one kind or another pursued many of the people associated with it. Saxon always said he bought it to keep him in his old age but that all it succeeded in doing was to ruin his middle years. He also said it was haunted, perhaps by the ghosts of those who had been tortured in the days when it was the Spanish Barracks, perhaps by the taxi-driver who had been murdered there (the driver's cap was still in one of the back rooms when Saxon took the house over), perhaps by the child who used the tiny crutch we found one day in the attic.

VII

It was in the St. Charles Hotel in New Orleans that Saxon spent much of the last twelve years of his life, and it was against this background that most of the people who came to call in those years saw him. In his last two years the room was filled with the relics of a somewhat diffused life. Visitors opening the door and expecting just a hotel room got a shock.

It was a large old-fashioned room with high ceilings. There were bookshelves on either side of the entrance filled with books that had accumulated during his stay at the hotel. They were not really representative of his taste or interests, however; most of the books he prized were in the cabin at Melrose. Then there was a screen, behind

JOE GILMORE USING AN ABSINTHE DRIPPER TO MAKE A FRAPPE

which, in Saxon's last year, the ever-attentive Joe Gilmore cooked breakfast, and in front of this an umbrella stand filled with canes which Saxon started to collect, or rather, which everyone showered on him when he developed a bad knee. These included several sword canes and one that had concealed inside of it a long hollow tube for liquor. An old armoire, which he had recently bought in one of the New Orleans shops, an antique desk he had had for many years, a beautifully finished sea chest with a secret drawer, and an old portable desk that also had a secret drawer were among the furnishings.

On a Nubian pedestal, which Bill Spratling had sent him from Mexico, was one of Saxon's prizes—a Negro banjo boy—a mechanical toy made in Europe and imported by some early planter for his child. The banjo boy, when wound up, strummed the banjo, moved his head and mouth and rolled his eyes, while a music box concealed in his stomach played a pleasant, unidentifiable tune. He had been elaborately dressed once, though when Saxon acquired him, some of his trappings had disappeared or were torn or tarnished; but he was still an impressive figure with his black tights, striped waistcoat, red satin jacket, and jeweled slippers.

The pictures were various. A huge fruit and flower still life done in a lush and realistic style, so much so that you could almost taste the grapes and cantaloupes, hung on the rear wall. A much smaller painting showed a mother centaur nursing her young, while the proud father centaur held up in the background a lion cub he had caught for their amusement. It was quite old and in the style of the German primitives. There was a colored lithograph of Toussaint-L'Ouverture, one of the many prints of Negro subjects that Saxon had collected, a drawing of the Madison Street house by Edward Suydam, and a wicked caricature of Saxon and Dreyer by Caroline Durieux, whom he long ago had nicknamed "the girl Goya."

But the picture that inevitably attracted the most attention was a large and elaborately framed work by Charles LeBrun, court painter to Louis XIV, called *Cupid with the Attributes of Love*. It had come from France through various ownerships into the collection of Sir Hobert Meyer. After the death of his widow, Adele, Lady Meyer, the paintings were sold by order of her heirs; this one eventually turned up in New Orleans, where Saxon acquired it. It was supposed to be a portrait of one of Louis' bastards. A sophisticated face, no longer young but crowned with golden curls, topped the rosy body of cupid—quite naked and quite male—who reclined against a background of elaborate red draperies. In one upraised hand he grasped a laurel wreath and the darts of love; from the other, held languidly at his side, poured pearls and multi-colored jewels; his feet rested carelessly on the open pages of a book of love sonnets. Off in the distance, in one corner and seen through a division in the draperies, a nymph and a satyr were doing an indelicate dance. The whole was executed with considerable flourish in the pompous style of the period.

Saxon always said he used it to help him judge people who came to call on him for the first time. If they did not notice it, they were hardly very perceptive. If they thought it was "perfectly beautiful" or took it too seriously, they were certainly lacking in humor. But if they burst into laughter, he knew he had something in common with them. One of the best comments was made by John Dos Passos who, peering at the picture through his thick glasses said: "My God! Is that a portrait of Lyle's appendix?"

Even the most unperceptive visitor could not fail to notice Grandpa's bed, a handsomely carved four-poster which Saxon had in storage for many years but moved into the hotel in the last two years of his life. He had new wine-red curtains and covers and a *ciel-de-lit* made for the bed. It was an astonishing thing to see in a hotel room.

Of course there were endless odds and ends which Saxon delighted to show people and about each of which he could tell some story: absinthe drippers and old carnival invitations, files of prints and photographs, a collection of phonograph records that contained some rare items from Rampart Street as well as a wide variety of odd recordings—offstage effects (so that he could have rain and wind and thunder if the occasion demanded), strange oriental music, early New Orleans jazz, and sad numbers from the twenties.

Then there were items reserved for those who had a special kind of humor. One was a collection of bad poetry. I remember a volume by a highly respected and capable physician in which each poem dealt with a disease, the high-point being the last two lines of the one on epilepsy:

> Will she ever get well? Will the spells ever cease?
> How little we know of the sacred disease!

Reserved for a very few people whom he knew quite well was a scrapebook called *Upsey-Daisy: A book for*

Little Tots by Miss Phillips." It had been started with Mrs. Lyons and various people contributed items which she would paste in. Eventually, however, she tired of it, as one does of a whimsey, and sent it back to Saxon, who added further chapters. It was a book of pictures, clippings, headlines, verses, and drawings—all scrambled together in weird or hilarious incongruity.

There was also a "crank file," since Saxon was the recipient of many extraordinary letters from a wide variety of people. He used to say he attracted crazy people. I suppose the truth of the matter was that he attracted all kinds of people because he was always interested in them. He would tell them amusing stories, feed them endless Bourbon, lend them money, or help them find jobs. But most important of all he would listen to their troubles. Weeks Hall once wrote about Saxon: "You could go to him about things. Literally thousands of people went to him about things." Out of the multitude who came by there were bound to be a number of eccentrics. They wrote him letters on an infinite number of subjects. Here is one of the many:

> New Orleans, Louisiana
> Friday, July the twenty-fourth, nineteen-forty-two

Mr. Lyle Saxon

Dear Mr. Saxon:

Since the last time I wrote to you I became a medium. Mr. Christy thinks it is merely another one of my money schemes, but it is not. Actually I can read minds and request immediate motional visions which appear on walls.

Through my communications with Jesus Christ, Virgin Mary, Saint Agnes, Mrs. Clare C. Williamson and a deceased aunt of mine, Mrs. Beatrice May Howard, I am a religious sleeping, reading, and visionary medium. I can also determine the characters of people by studying their photographs.

A copy of one of the forms we intend to use is enclosed.

Yours gratefully

E. Peters

Medium in Charge

of

Moses Academy

New Orleans, Louisiana

Moses Academy

The House of the Children of God

Specializing In

The Reading of The Mind

By Religious Medium

Of the Past—Present—Future

Prayers Offered

For the Souls of the Dead

And for All

Earthly Human Problems

Life Readings

$5.00

Special Readings

$1.00

Donations are accepted for the rebuilding of a school

One of Saxon's favorite stories of his career in the St. Charles concerned a period when he had been drinking heavily and was threatening to swear off. Always, however, a new group of old friends (or a new group of new friends) would turn up and there would be another evening of conviviality. Then one night, he said, the bad thing happened.

He was finally, after a long heavy evening, alone. Getting into bed, he immediately dozed off. But suddenly he was awake and looking down at the foot of his bed, saw a large white cat. Thinking he must be dreaming, he blinked his eyes hard and opened them again. The cat was no longer there, but as he looked around the dimly lit room, he saw it sitting in an armchair. Fully awake now, and on the jittery side, he began to say to himself: "I know I should have stopped before this. It's come now, it's come at last. This is it, Saxon." Then he closed his eyes and shook his head again. When he opened them the cat was no longer in the chair. Probably sitting on my left shoulder, he thought and, summoning all his courage, let his eyes once more travel around the room. No, the cat was not on his left shoulder. This time it was standing, with its back arched and tail erect, on the desk at the other end of the room.

"Oh, Lord," Saxon said, "please make it go away. I'll stop, I promise. Just don't let me see the cat again." He was about to add a great many more equally rash promises when he heard a commotion in the hall outside. There were the voices of two men and then the voice of a woman saying: "Here kitty, kitty, here kitty." Then there was a knock on the door and Milton Tabary and Sidney Gab both bell-hops and both devoted friends of Saxon were saying almost in unison: "We hope you're not asleep. We hate to disturb you; but this lady's lost a cat. Have you seen anything of a large white cat?" Saxon bounded from his bed, put on a dressing gown and opened the door. "We're awfully sorry," Milton and Sidney began again. "You must forgive us," said the lady, and added, "Minerva, you wicked girl!" as the cat came bounding toward her.

There were more apologies; but eventually Milton, Sidney, the lady, and the cat were gone. Saxon was again alone in his room. He sat down in an armchair and poured himself a very stiff drink.

Saxon had an ability to make comebacks after a heavy bout of drinking with amazing rapidity. His energy was always something that left younger, and from all appearances tougher, people panting to keep up with him. I remember one particularly strenuous week end when there were even more people passing through the Saxon *ménage* than usual and an even larger amount of Bourbon than usual was consumed. Knowing that Saxon had a speaking engagement in Baton Rouge, Monday evening, I told him he had better go easy or he'd fall flat on his well-known face. He said he would be all right and to prove it would send me a wire after the speech. The speech was quite a success and was enthusiastically reviewed in the Baton Rouge papers. But late Monday night my telephone rang. It was the girl night operator in the small town where I was stationed, giggling as she read a telegram which was signed by Miss Essae M. Culver, Head of the Louisiana Library Commission, and Ella V. Aldrich (Mrs. Calvin Schwing) old friends of Saxon. There was no doubt, however, that Saxon himself had composed it. It read:

SAXON'S SPEECH GREAT SUCCESS. ENTIRELY INCOMPREHENSIBLE. HE ONLY FELL DOWN TWICE. THOUGHT YOU SHOULD KNOW.

VIII

No one has written of the New Orleans Mardi Gras with more insight than Lyle Saxon. Those who do not know the first chapter of his *Fabulous New Orleans* should try it for its account of a child's impression of that mad and fantastic day. Much of the chapter, he said, was autobiographical and tells, in part, his own experiences as a child when his grandfather brought him from Baton Rouge to New Orleans.

For many years as a reporter he covered the Mardi Gras —the usual elaborate preliminary festivites as well as the merrymaking throughout the entire city on Mardi Gras day itself. On his own he sometimes masked with a group known as the "Bourbon Street Bounders" and he used to recall one season in particular when a debutante, pushed by her family into being queen of more balls than were good for her, was celebrated in a song that began: "Please don't make me Queen of Comus, Papa."

Eventually, he was worn out with reporting the carnival. He had long been bored with its social pretensions. By 1935 he was no longer going to any of the balls (as far as I know he never again went to one) and he did not mask on Mardi Gras day. His secretary, Katie, who came from Mississippi, had never masked, but that year she joined a group representing three blind mice and the farmer's wife. With a butcher's knife in one hand and part of a bloody mousetail in the other, Katie was a great success.

That night after the Comus ball we had supper with Saxon. Hazel Breaux, who had been one of the blind mice, declared that there were fewer maskers than she had ever seen and that most of those who were masked seemed to have used little imagination. If anybody could do something about this, surely Saxon could. Early Ash Wednesday

LYLE SAXON AT A TOMB ON GRAND ISLE
The Chighizolas were among those who, with Lafitte, the Pirate, helped Jackson
win the Battle of New Orleans.

morning, over a final Sazerac, Saxon was agreeing to try to do something about it.

Every year thereafter until the war, he wrote, for several weeks before Mardi Gras day, a column urging people to mask and describing costumes and incidents of past Mardi Gras'. The response was very gratifying. Letters poured in from old friends and perfect strangers, natives and tourists, the high and the mighty, the lowly and the undistinguished. Saxon's daily mail became a wild collection of communications from ex-queens of carnival and truck drivers, French Quarter drunks and deans of universities, old ladies who had arrived the day before from Kansas and little girls let loose from their convent in Opelousas. Those who never before had the courage to mask now did; and they had a wonderful time.

Saxon himself masked thereafter, usually with Joel Lawrence. Once he was Bluebeard and she was Puss-in-Boots. Once he was a particularly vicious-looking were-wolf and she was Marguerite, quite pregnant after that unfortunate experience with Faust. Once they were Dalmatian coach hounds carrying large bunches of artificial forsythia. Saxon explained this accessory as follows: They found identical papier mâché dog faces in a French Quarter shop and a local seamstress concocted dog costumes using smelly shoe dye to paint the spots. The day before Mardi Gras, Joel came by for a dress rehearsal. They were both pleased with their appearance but Saxon felt that they needed something else to give them true dash and style. To have the dogs carry bunches of artificial dogwood blossoms seemed just the thing. He started out for the ten-cent store; but on his way he met Ike Stauffer who seduced him into the Sazerac Bar; after that he met Pierre Durieux; after that Clair Laning and Dick Foster and Bob Crager and Mike O'Leary and Robert Tallant and Thad St. Martin; after that he met someone else. When he finally arrived at the counter where artifical flowers were sold, he was more than a little vague. So he came away with a large armful of yellow flowers which suddenly caught his eye. It was just as well. The forsythia simply added one more bizarre note.

On every Mardi Gras—as, indeed, on practically every day of the year—Saxon's room at the St. Charles was definitely "Grand Hotel." People came and people went, and a hell of a lot of things happened. Eventually, in order to relieve the congestion on Mardi Gras, he joined forces with Mrs. Douglas, who lived on the same floor and who also had her guest problems. Parties of the kind described in *The Friends of Joe Gilmore* were the result.

But Saxon's delight in the fantastic was, like that of many Orleanians, not limited to one day in the year. For a number of years there were small masquerade parties on Hallowe'en to which he added much merriment. Some of his friends will remember him with glee as a combination of Little Lord Fauntleroy and Mr. Hyde—six feet three and two hundred and forty pounds—in blond curls and knee britches, but with hideously protruding artificial eyes, tusks for teeth, and hairy clawlike hands. On another occasion he arrived back from Washington too late to get a costume. So he stopped his cab at a bakery on the way and made a triumphal entrance as "The Staff of Life," with a turban designed from a round loaf of Italian bread topped by a hotdog bun, a necklace of doughnuts, and a sceptre of

French bread ornamented with cream puffs and chocolate eclairs. To the last of these parties before the war, he came as Rasputin, particularly appalling in a beard and a bald and diseased-looking scalp with a narrow fringe of dirty hair. With him was Joel, wearing a red wig, an artificial nose, a sleazy velvet evening dress rubbed shiny at the most prominent parts of her anatomy, and much costume jewelry. Her right arm was in a sling. As they entered, Saxon gave it a yank; out it came and he began to gnaw at the bloody meat tied to the end.

During the war there was no Mardi Gras, and the first one after the war (1946) was his last. Not being very well, he did not mask; he did, however, make several radio broadcasts and his room as usual on Mardi Gras was filled with friends who came by to show off their costumes, and to wish him health and wealth and a great many more such days. But he was a sick man, and had been for the last three years. Shortly after he was back in the hospital. While there he had one more good laugh in the foolish Mardi Gras tradition he always loved.

A number of years before, while checking some information concerning Grande Isle, we found, in a trash heap behind an old cemetery, a discarded funeral wreath of leaves and grasses made of tin. Carted back to New Orleans it served various purposes until one day, when Saxon was not feeling well, it was gilded and presented to him with ceremony. Several years later, when Joel broke her leg, he went to see her in the hospital and brought her the same wreath. During his last illness, Joel, not knowing how sick Saxon was, but knowing that no matter what his condition he would always enjoy a laugh, got herself fixed up as a

Creole widow with a black dress, black stockings, black gloves and a heavy black veil. She painted her face dead white and used colorless nail polish in splotches on her cheeks to simulate tears. Carelessly wrapping the wreath in a torn newspaper, she made her appearance at the hospital. No one recognized her, but everyone was very sympathetic. She was carefully helped into the elevator and allowed in the Saxon room where entrance had been denied most visitors. Then, pointing a black-gloved finger at Saxon and displaying the wreath with the other hand, she cried out in a voice that was not her own: "Have they found the will yet?" For a few seconds even Saxon did not recognize her. When he did, he laughed heartily and insisted that she visit six other friends who also happened to be in the hospital at the moment.

On April 9, 1946, Lyle Saxon died in New Orleans. He was buried in Magnolia Cemetery, Baton Rouge, Louisiana.

Of the many tributes since paid to him perhaps none pleased his friends more than that inserted by George Sessions Perry in the "Personals" column of the New Orleans newspapers for April 17:

> Since it is an old New Orleans custom to print one's feelings in religious manners, and since Lyle Saxon so deeply favored each of these old customs, I'd like to burn this one small candle of congratulations to God Almighty, who now has the rich, the easy, yet exquisite pleasure of the company of this lonely, generous man.